"A very useful contribution to the people's understanding of the mystery of the Eucharist."

— Most Rev. Malcolm McMahon, OP
Archbishop of Liverpool

"A beautiful book, as accessible as it is profound. I have learned much and gained even more."

— Prof. Stephen Bullivant
Institute of Theology, St. Mary's University, Twickenham

"May the present book of Rev. Fr. de Malleray, FSSP, a beautiful and impressive '*paper* shrine to the Most Holy Eucharist,' have a wide diffusion and be a practical spiritual aid in order to renew the Catholic Faith, the Catholic love, and the Catholic worship of the Sacrament of the Most Holy Eucharist."

— + Athanasius Schneider
Auxiliary Bishop of the Archdiocese of
Saint Mary in Astana

"Sometimes the language and concepts surrounding the Eucharistic Mystery can be difficult or impenetrable for many people. Fr. Armand de Malleray has a gift for explaining traditional doctrine and practice without losing anything in depth or precision. In a lively, innovative, and engaging style, Ego Eimi – *It Is I* passes on the timeless treasures of traditional Catholic Faith and is a great service to the Church."

— Fr. Marcus Holden
Author of the *Evangelium* catechetical series

"The Holy Eucharist is a sublime mystery before which it is often better to remain in silent adoration than to attempt to open one's mouth in explanation. And yet where would we be without the great writings of the saints on this Sacrament, which is rightly and truly called 'the Most Blessed'? All the more today do we need authors who can help us *see* with fresh amazement the miracle of Our Lord's Real Presence in our midst and to hunger for the unique, unsurpassable nourishment He offers us from the altar of the Cross. In this book, Fr. de Malleray has given us a vivid introduction to the 'font and apex of the Christian life,' with unexpected angles and brilliant connections that refresh an old subject for contemporary readers. May it bring the minds and hearts of many readers nearer to 'the bread of God that cometh down from heaven, and giveth life to the world.'"

—Dr. Peter Kwasniewski
Author of *Noble Beauty, Transcendent Holiness:
Why the Modern Age Needs the Mass of Ages*

"This highly readable, informative, and edifying treatise on the Holy Eucharist will enrich the understanding and devotion of Catholics regardless of their prior knowledge of the subject: I recommend it wholeheartedly."

—Dr. Joseph Shaw, Ph.D.
Chairman of the Latin Mass Society

"I heartily recommend this book to all."

—Very Rev. John M. Berg, FSSP
Former Superior General of
the Priestly Fraternity of St. Peter

Ego Eimi—It Is I

Fr. Armand de Malleray, FSSP

Ego Eimi — It Is I
Falling in Eucharistic Love

SOPHIA INSTITUTE PRESS
Manchester, New Hampshire

Imprimi potest: Very Rev. John M. Berg, FSSP,
Superior General, FSSP, Fribourg, June 5, 2018

Nihil obstat: Very Rev. Msgr. Peter Fleetwood,
Censor Deputatus, Liverpool, July 30, 2018

Imprimatur: Most Rev. Malcolm McMahon, OP,
Archbishop of Liverpool, Liverpool, July 30, 2018

Sophia Institute Press
Box 5284, Manchester, NH 03108
1-800-888-9344

www.SophiaInstitute.com

Sophia Institute Press is a registered trademark of Sophia Institute.

paperback ISBN 978-1-64413-670-6

ebook ISBN 978-1-64413-671-3

Library of Congress Control Number: 2021952751

First printing

Contents

Foreword

The Holy Eucharist is the sacrament of the divine love. It is the sacrament of faith. The Eucharist is the greatest of all the miracles that Christ ever wrought. The Eucharist is the greatest consolation that God has given us here on Earth, in this valley of tears. Indeed, the Eucharist is not a sacred thing; the Eucharist is the Lord Himself. It is the Lord: *Dominus est*! He is here present truly, really, and substantially with His Body, Blood, Soul, and Divinity.

In his reflections on the Sacrament of the Most Holy Eucharist, with the significant title Ego Eimi – *It Is I*, Rev. Fr. Armand de Malleray, FSSP, made a precious spiritual gift to the priests and to the faithful of our time. In his book, he shows that the Sacrament of the Most Holy Eucharist is not only a holy thing but it is ultimately the Person of Our Lord and Savior, Jesus Christ, who revealed His infinite love in the most deep, striking, and loving manner in that sacrament.

Rev. Fr. de Malleray presents us with reflections upon the Most Holy Eucharist, which are born from the knowledge of the sacred Faith and from the consequent experience of this Faith in celebrating and receiving this divine Sacrament.

In the midst of the spiritual ruins by which the Eucharistic life in the Church of our days is largely characterized, we have to renew the true Catholic Faith. Rev. Fr. de Malleray rightly wrote in the introduction to his book: "We have our Catholic Faith. It is all we need, for now, for the scattered stones to assemble and for pillars and arches to rise afresh in our souls." One has first to know Our Lord in the depth of His ineffable Eucharistic Sacrament. Such knowledge, illuminated by the Faith, impels us to love the Eucharistic Lord ever more. The true love for the Eucharistic Lord then necessarily demands exterior gestures of awe and respect.

May this book of Rev. Fr. de Malleray, a beautiful and impressive "*paper* shrine to the Most Holy Eucharist," have a wide diffusion and be a practical spiritual aid in order to renew the Catholic Faith, the Catholic love, and the Catholic worship of the Sacrament of the Most Holy Eucharist. Let us "have a great love for Jesus in His divine sacrament of love. That is the divine oasis of the desert. It is the heavenly manna of the traveler. It is the Holy Ark. It is the life and paradise of love on earth."[1]

— + Athanasius Schneider
Auxiliary Bishop of the Archdiocese
of Saint Mary in Astana
Sunday, June 17, 2018

---

[1] St. Peter Julian Eymard, To the Children of Mary, November 21, 1851.

Introduction

The beautiful ruins of Basingwerk Abbey still stand in Welsh Flintshire, looking toward England over the estuary of the River Dee and across the Irish Sea, toward the Emerald Isle. For years, on my visits to the former abbey, I mistook the refectory for the monastic church. But a closer look at the drawing on the visitors' board enlightened me. That vast room, well preserved, was where the monks would meet thrice a day to restore their bodies, sitting at tables. On the opposite side of the cloister, they would gather in the church to feed their souls through worship, seven times a day.

Not much is left of the church, compared with the other conventual buildings, such as the chapter room, the dormitories, the kitchen, the infirmary, and the stores. And yet the church was by far the most important part of the abbey. Admittedly, the monks would not only eat in the refectory. They would also pray there, saying grace. Reciprocally, in the chapel, they would not only pray but also be fed with the "bread of heaven," the Most Holy Eucharist.

My latest visit to Basingwerk was on a fine afternoon in spring. A couple of families were picnicking, sitting on the steps of the lay brothers' crumbled dormitory. At the other end of the ruins, a man was throwing a ball to his dog, which ran along the former church nave toward the area where, long ago, the altar would have stood. Did the monks of old have community picnics? Did they have dogs? From Heaven, where one would hope they now stood or knelt, surely the monks would be blessing the nice families, the man and his dog (why not?), and even me. What would they wish us, according to our respective conditions? The latest strollers? A puppy to train? A new ball to chew? Italian vestments? More parishioners?

Through all these and beyond, they would wish us to fall in love. Which love? The love of God-made-Man, who promised humankind that He would be with us each day until the consummation of the world. They would wish us to become intoxicated with joy. Which joy? That joy springing from Christ's true presence in the Holy Eucharist—in every Catholic church, in every tabernacle. They would wish us to experience the peace secured in God's true presence on Earth, offered in the Holy Eucharist to every man, woman, and child.

Why had their church roof, walls, and pillars collapsed? Why was the altar gone, and, around such a hallowed spot where the priest would have trodden in awe, why was the holy of holies now discernible only through greener grass and taller dandelions? Had the Vikings razed the abbey? No, since it was built after they had left or converted. Then, were the arches and buttresses poorly designed in the first place, after the modern fashion, which doesn't last? No, since those segments of walls left untouched still stood high, after nearly one thousand years.

The *cold* had brought the place to naught. What cold? It was the cold in the hearts of Catholics enamored with created goods and comfortable opinions, and grown oblivious of their loving Creator and Savior. Tampering with the Faith handed down from the Apostles (that Faith witnessed to by countless martyrs and radiated through the virtues of millions of simple and learned believers), a new generation came to ignore God's true presence in the Holy Eucharist and soon denied it. For clergy and laity alike, fidelity to this most salutary belief was then condemned as *high treason*. After centuries of "superstition," the age of "reason" had dawned—so they were told. When the last sanctuary lamp was smashed, the dazzling constellation of churches large and small across the land—from country chapels to city minsters—was snuffed out. No longer would souls gather around the warmth of the tabernacles. No more would they swallow the glowing *charcoal* shared from the Eucharistic furnace, the altar of sacrifice. To save their lives, most would claim that they didn't feel the cold or that "it never bothered them anyway."

We were born after them. In this third millennium, regardless of where we live, are we Catholics still shivering, or are we frozen outright? Do we hold firm and clear in our minds the Eucharistic truths; and if so, do our hearts hunger and thirst for the divine sustenance? Or was that dog in Basingwerk's Abbey church more eager to catch in its mouth its master's ball, than we our Savior's Gift? How fast do we run to the Sacred Host? How often? How lovingly? And when we come to church, do we understand that brotherliness within the congregation can stem only from Christ's Sacrifice, or do we think Holy Mass is a family picnic?

Geographically, the ruins of Basingwerk Abbey lie within the fence of a small field in Flintshire. Spiritually, though, are they not scattered all over the world, wherever the Eucharistic faith has grown cold? Even where church buildings stand apparently firm, are they more than floating dust if the Eucharistic Lord — the Host to whom all men are guests — is not sought in their sanctuaries? Not listened to? Not trusted? Not adored? Looking at such doctrinal, liturgical, and devotional ruins, we may decide not to care, thinking it too late, or not worth it, or too challenging. But we may also try to restore them.

We may have neither money nor architectural skills, but we have our catechism. We have our Catholic Faith. It is all we need, for now, for the scattered stones to assemble and for pillars and arches to rise afresh in our souls. We can rebuild or improve our *interior* churches, welcoming our Eucharistic God in the tabernacles of our hearts, within the shrines of our minds. Dear reader, for want of stones and marble, let us use paper — let us hold a pen rather than a trowel, and ink instead of mortar. As to stain glass, it will come separately.

This little book could thus be seen as a *paper* shrine to the Most Holy Eucharist. Chapters 1 and 2, "Solving the 'Chrisham Complex'?" and "Radiations through Lenses," are the narthex or entrance to the building. They adjust the perspective from a psychological point of view to that of the Christian revelation.

Chapters 3 through 7 figure the nave of the building. Thus, chapter 3, "The Transubstantiation," defines what is at stake. Chapter 4, "The Holy Eucharist as Judgment," shows how the Holy Eucharist applies to our earthly lives in anticipation of eternity. Chapter 5, "Gradation of the Modes of Presence," provides a criterion to assess the Eucharistic presence. A homily rather than an essay, chapter 6, "Who Says 'Hocus Pocus'?", examines the claim for the power to transubstantiate. Chapter 7, "*Eleison!* The Latin Mass in One Greek Word," describes the context in which the Holy Eucharist occurs—namely, the Holy Sacrifice of the Mass.

Having, by then, walked down the nave of our paper shrine, we reach the transept, that is, the two left and right arms of the cross-shaped building. Thus, chapter 8, "Eucharistic Fragments," explains the practical implications of Christ's presence in the Sacred Host. Symmetrically, chapter 9, "On Concomitance: 'Is Christ Divided?'"—shows the extent of Christ's presence, both in the Sacred Host and in the Chalice.

With chapter 10, the longest of all, we properly enter the sanctuary. "The Formulas of Consecration" offers a detailed examination of the words printed in the missal, of those words as spoken by the priest, and of the gestures he performs as vehicles of the divine power and as guidance for the congregation to adhere in faith to the Eucharistic change. We may call this topic the *nuclear reactor* of the Eucharistic mystery.

Finally, the two last chapters represent the ambulatory of our paper church, surrounding the rear of the sanctuary. Our brief chapter 11, "Holy Mass as the Measure of Motion," aims at gathering the accumulated Eucharistic considerations into one simple perspective. The final chapter, "Light the Beacons!" in a style proper to a homily, connects the Holy Eucharist with the priesthood and states the reasons why optimism is essential to Catholicism.

To the Mother of God, the Immaculate Virgin Mary who gave us the Savior, her Son, I submit these illuminations, colored with a clumsy paintbrush. May their imperfections not hinder our readers but, rather, inspire them to see for themselves what Holy Church teaches in her catechisms and sound theology. I offer these reflections to any lovers of the Holy Eucharist; to our dear young adults in particular; and to all fellow Catholics.

"Blessed be Jesus in the Most Holy Sacrament of the Altar!"

St. Mary's Shrine Church, Warrington
Corpus Christi 2018

1

Solving the "Chrisham Complex"?

A Tale of Two Lads

"Say what's behind!" Two lads are playing in the backyard, where their mother is hanging the bedsheets on a line to dry. For a game, they describe to each other what they think lies behind the white material. Chris says that "behind" is a continent to discover. On the contrary, Ham says that "behind" is a threat to fear. Pretending to hold a telescope before his eye, Chris now insists that, surely, behind the sheet are wonderful people to meet and riches to share. But Ham picks up a stick and directs it at the white sheet as a sword, being adamant that evil is hiding behind and should be crushed if possible. Taller than the boys, Mummy smiles, since she can see what stands "behind" the sheet—it is their home.

The lads Chris and Ham grow up and die, remaining familiar to us as Christopher Columbus and Hamlet of Denmark. We only imagined their meeting, of course, because their lives offer suggestive parallels. Both men belong to illustrious nations of navigators (Genoa and Denmark); both fall from grace with a queen (Isabel and Gertrude); both are thought insane; both benefit from an eclipse (obtaining food in Jamaica; meeting with the ghost at Elsinore).

But let us focus on a crucial occasion in their lives, when both stood as grown men before hanging material. On board the *Santa Maria*, Columbus called the hanging a *sail*. He prayed for fair winds to blow in it so as to reach India. In his mother's room, Hamlet stabbed Polonius through the tapestry, claiming it was a rat. Columbus meant to serve his Mother the Church and the Spanish Crown, bringing the gospel to yet unevangelized souls. Hamlet distrusted his mother, the adulterous queen. He meant to kill the usurper king, but instead, he ruined his chance of happiness with the orphaned Ophelia.

We obviously simplify these two destinies, offering them as types of two contrasted attitudes in relation to what lies "behind." It seems to us that all men admit that there is a "behind." They only differ in the response they give about it. Some fear what is behind and wish to destroy it. Others seek it as an opportunity, as a calling—as a grace.

Either we are like Columbus, or we are like Hamlet. Columbus looks at what appears and tries to meet what is behind. On board his caravel, he looks at his sail filling and believes that a passage to India lies behind it. His intention may not be wholly disinterested, and his achievement may not be without flaws. But he assumes that what lies behind is good for mankind and can and should be reached by him. He flies there—*Columbus* is Latin for "a male dove."

On the contrary, Hamlet distrusts the signs perceived through the tapestry. In his mother's room, he hears a voice and stabs the man standing behind, hoping to kill the usurper, but in vain. Claudius lives on, Polonius lies dead, and Hamlet's position is made worse. His suspicious outlook on life makes him feel trapped in a shrinking world. *Hamlet* means "a small village" (without a church). Hamlet lacks the courage and faith to reach out to what lies "behind." He fails and brings others down in his fall.

A mere contraction of the names of Christopher Columbus and Hamlet, our "Chrisham Complex" encapsulates two truths. The first truth is that all men admit there is a "behind." The second truth is that "behind" attracts some as a promise and repels others as a threat. These considerations can help us look afresh at the Holy Eucharist.

Catholics do nothing strange or irrational when their souls profess the true presence of God where their eyes see only bread. Simply, they look at the externals of the Host as at a wrapping. The color, the taste, the smell of the Host express that a Gift—not a threat—awaits our soul "behind" what appears. That Gift is wider than a new continent, more savory than all the spices of India, and more valuable than gold and gems. That Gift is God-made-Man, Jesus Christ, truly present with His Sacred Body, His Precious Blood, His human soul, and His divinity.

Thus, at the beginning of this little book, each of us stands closer either to Chris or to Ham. The good news is that we need not oppose the two stances. Ham has everything to gain in coming closer to Chris, and so do we. During Holy Mass, as we gaze at the whitish surface of the sacred Host in the hands of the priest, we can learn not to fear the unthinkable possibility. Which one? That our eyes see bread while our mind holds God to be truly there, behind.

To Be or Not to Be

Let us not assume that any believer understands perfectly the Eucharistic mystery. On the contrary, one's Eucharistic faith is called to grow year after year, as we learn the complex but very logical doctrines that shed light on this mystery, as upon a garden explored through various vistas. God's garden is large—so our promenade may take a bit longer than a stroll—but is rich in fragrances and colors, thankfully. I invite the reader to join us on this journey of discovery.

The various essays gathered in this volume are not a systematic and scholarly presentation. They merely aim at offering third-millennium readers an entry into the Eucharistic truths. To that end, I will borrow examples from modern life and will use metaphors. A little precision may be fitting at this stage. While comparisons and analogies are useful to grasp theological truths, they should not be mistaken for the truth they refer to. When, with the Church, we say that the Host *is* the Body of Christ, we mean it literally, not metaphorically. When, with the Church, we say that the Chalice contains the Precious Blood of Christ, we mean it literally, not metaphorically.

Why is this important? Because long before Christ offered the First Mass in Jerusalem, in Athens Aristotle had discovered the law of noncontradiction. In *Metaphysics*, the Greek philosopher states, "For the same thing to be present and not be present at the same time in the same subject, and according to the same, is impossible." This law of noncontradiction is one of the first principles of knowledge. It is a prerequisite to any science, including natural and social sciences, not only theological ones.

Applied to the Holy Eucharist, it means either that Christ's Body, Blood, Soul, and Divinity *are* present for real—or that they are *not* present for real. By "present," I mean a fact as concrete and objective as the reader's fingers on the page of this book, or his eyes reading these words. Even though I may use metaphors, I am writing not for metaphorical readers but for readers of flesh and blood, objectively present there and then. The reality of their existence is admitted by all in a rational society. We claim the same objectiveness for the reality of God's presence in the Holy Eucharist. If God is there, then His presence concerns every human, whether each one knows it yet or not. It cannot be true for some and false for others. Either Catholics are mistaken and unbelievers are right, or unbelievers are mistaken and Catholics are right. One group can be misinformed or in denial while the other group truly grasps the matter, but both groups cannot be right about the Holy Eucharist at the same time.

The One Who Is

Through Holy Scripture and through His Church, God Himself tells us about Himself. God is the only being who has not received His existence from another. On the contrary, God grants existence to all other beings. In God only, essence (what He is) and existence (the fact that He is) coincide. This is the meaning of His revelation to Moses, from the burning bush: "Moses said to God: Lo, I shall go to the children of Israel, and say to them: The God of your fathers hath sent me to you. If they should say to me: What is his name? what shall I say to them? God said to Moses: I AM WHO AM. He said: Thus shalt thou say to the children of Israel: HE WHO IS hath sent me to you" (Exod. 3:13–14).

In St. John's Gospel alone, Jesus Himself says "I am" (Greek: *ego eimi*) twenty-four times.[2] He speaks emphatically

---

[2] According to Felix Just, SJ, Ph.D.

11

in these instances, explicitly including the pronoun "I" (Greek: *ego*), which would not be necessary in Greek grammar. Nine of these are emphatic absolute, with no predicate. For example, when He asked the soldiers and guards who had come to arrest Him in the Garden of Gethsemane whom they were seeking, "they answered him, 'Jesus of Nazareth.' Jesus said to them, 'I am he.' Judas, who betrayed him, was standing with them. When he said to them, 'I am he,' they drew back and fell to the ground" (John 18:5-6, RSVCE).[3] There is no doubt that on those occasions Jesus states His divinity in the strongest manner, despite the fact that it remains veiled behind His humanity.

In another occurrence, Jesus states that He is bread, to be eaten up. When the crowds understand His word literally and are scandalized, He does not correct them: "Jesus said to them: 'I am the bread of life: he that cometh to me shall not hunger: and he that believeth in me shall never thirst.' ... The Jews therefore murmured at him, because he had said: 'I am the bread which came down from heaven.' ... 'I am the bread of life.... I am the living bread which came down from heaven; if any one eats of this bread, he will live for ever; and the bread which I shall give for the life of the world is my flesh'" (see John 6:35, 41, 48, 51-52).

When, on Maundy Thursday, the Lord Jesus instituted the Holy Eucharist, He spoke literally, as the Church always understood it: "And taking bread, he gave thanks, and brake; and gave to them, saying: This is my body, which is given

---

[3] The RSV and other English Bibles often translate this phrase, "I am he," but the pronoun "he" is not explicit in the Greek text.

for you. Do this for a commemoration of me. In like manner the chalice also, after he had supped, saying: This is the chalice, the new testament in my blood, which shall be shed for you" (Luke 22:19-20). The One uttering those words in such a solemn moment is the same who revealed Himself to Moses as the One Who Is, by whose word everything else was created. The dogma of the Holy Eucharist makes no sense if God does not exist. But given God's existence, on what ground could His creatures deny Him the power to change bread and wine into His Body and Blood while concealing His presence under the externals of bread and wine? On the contrary, I will endeavor to show that the Eucharistic dogmas are beautifully consistent with the Catholic Faith as handed down to us across the centuries—further expounded but not altered.

I would be glad if the simple considerations I offer in the following chapters could embolden those who fear what is "behind." Fear need not be expressed through shivering and sweat. For something as mysterious and powerful as the Eucharistic dogma, the more likely symptom of fear could be irony and scorn—scorn for doctrines one refuses to take time to consider, for fear they may alter radically one's outlook on life, bringing challenges and calling for sacrifices. Instead, I hope that every reader will aspire to gain an empire like Columbus, rather than miss a throne like Hamlet. I pray that any reader standing near Ham will slowly come closer to Chris, trusting in the promise offered behind the veil, until one joy unites their souls. That is the way to solve the "Chrisham Complex."

2

Radiations through Lenses

On Pilgrimage to Italy

The pale disc was barely visible in the rising hands of the priest until it reached the sunray shining through the narrow window behind the altar. At that moment, the Host turned dazzling white above the head of the celebrant. The sun had just risen behind the nearby hills of San Cristoforo, and the abbey church was still almost dark, save for that beam sent by a distant star through that mere slot in the stone.

Our presence on the feast day of the local saint, Abbot Cristoforo of Montalcino, seemed fortuitous. On our way from Bavaria to Rome, we had traveled eight hours across the Swiss Alps, reaching the abbey the evening before, shortly after sunset. We meant to spend the night there, south of Parma. To our surprise, the narrow road leading from the village, uphill, to the medieval church down in the vale, was filled with hundreds of exuberant country folk carrying a statue and singing joyful canticles (or so we assumed, not understanding a word of the local dialect). We parked wherever we could and followed the happy crowd into the sacred building, only then realizing that our arrival coincided with San Cristoforo's festival. After various devotions (and much clapping), the worshippers dispersed. We could not turn down having a snack (mozzarella and local wine), before happily slipping into our beds at the guesthouse, weary from our long journey and grateful for having witnessed such colorful piety.

To Mass

We rose early. None of the villagers attended our Mass, which started before dawn. Probably the high Mass in honor of the saintly Abbot Cristoforo would take place later that morning, after our departure for Rome. We were but a dozen young men in our first year of training for the priesthood. After eight months in seminary, we knew very well that Holy Mass is the most important event in the world, every day.

What, then, is Holy Mass? It is the unbloody reenactment of the Sacrifice of Christ on Calvary. We also knew that the most important moment of Holy Mass is called the Consecration, when bread and wine are turned into the Body, Blood, Soul, and Divinity of God-made-Man, Jesus Christ, the Lord and Savior of all men.

Ding! Amid the pristine silence, the little bell rang at the Consecration. At the altar, the priest genuflected and, standing again, elevated the Host. In the dim candlelight, all eyes looked intently at the frail disc, slowly rising in the hands of the priest, until it met the sunbeam and instantaneously radiated solar light. The alignment of such diverse objects struck me: the sun, the Host, my eye. The sun was about ninety-three million miles away. In the hands of the priest, the sacred Host was only ten feet from where we knelt in the pews. How far were my heart and brain from my eye? A matter of inches. Then how fast would the light cast by the white disc reach my soul, through my optic nerve, channeled through the virtue of faith? It had taken slightly over eight minutes for the photons emitted by the sun to reach Earth—impressive, considering the distance traveled. The same photons had focused on northern Italy and reached the abbey window, the Host, and finally my eye. And next? Helpfully, the photons were now translated to my brain as nonvisual information soon communicated to my heart. Was my heart aligned, then, as my eye was with the Host and the sun? Did I *believe* that what I saw as bread in the hands of the priest standing at the altar—was God? Thank God, I did.

Some Architecture

If sunlight had touched the Host and our eyes, it was not by chance. As was explained to us, the abbey church of San Cristoforo had been designed so that, on the feast day of the local saint, the sun would rise exactly in the axis of the altar where Mass was offered. The architect had found such alignment significant. It revealed the sacred Host as the true Sun of Justice, Christ, rising from the East, as He will on His return at the end of time, to judge the living and the dead. Pagan temples in India, in Egypt, and in Central America had also made use of the rising sun to convey meaning.

Closer to us in time and history, the same feature was used at the French palace of Versailles. Experts believe that the magnificent buildings and its sumptuous gardens are orientated toward the point on the horizon where the sun sets on August 25, the feast of King St. Louis of France, ancestor and namesake of Louis XIV, the Sun King, who built Versailles. Recent measurements, however, show that the axis of the Grand Canal leads to a slightly different point on the horizon, corresponding to sunset ten days earlier, that is, on

August 15, the great Marian feast. Historians explain that Louis XIV must have chosen that date, rather than St. Louis's feast day, so as to honor the Blessed Virgin Mary on the feast of her Assumption. His father, King Louis XIII, had made a solemn vow establishing the Assumption as the national feast of France in perpetuity. Having remained without an heir for twenty-two years, and been caught in a difficult war, the sonless king begged Our Lady's intervention. He was heard that same year, 1637, when the Queen gave birth to Louis Dieudonné, the future Louis XIV.

Optical Metaphor

Let us return to Italy. On that morning, above the altar of San Cristoforo, the sun was right behind the Host. Both were so perfectly aligned that the priest seemed to be holding the star, rather than the wafer. What looked like bread seemed to contain a sun. How striking! But the sun is visible, although distant. Could the Host encompass nonvisible realities? Could meta- or infrasensorial data be circumscribed by the Host, just as the sun was aligned with it? Could we discover them? What is there *behind*?

The consecrated Host calls for such a question. The Church allows enquiry, as she distinguishes between what the Host looks like and what it really is. Its *surface*, so to speak, rightly appears as bread to our eyes of flesh (although it is not bread). The *inside*, that is, the reality behind what appears, is the Sacred Body of Christ, made perceptible to our soul through the prism of faith.

Let us now go back to the sun. We know stars through their light. When we analyze their light, we know their chemical composition. Spectroscopy is the study of spectral lines from atoms and is applied to stars and interstellar clouds. Could we have a spectroscopic analysis of the Host? Using the right prism, could we split its light into its component colors, so as to discover its nonsensorial elements?

The Church teaches that under the externals of bread (and wine), Christ is truly, really, and substantially present with His Sacred Body, His Precious Blood, His human Soul, and His Divinity. But we will appreciate better why and how those four actual components are invisibly present if we use a dogmatic prism or spectroscope to guide our meditation.

Our proposed apparatus comprises three pairs of lenses aligned. The three pairs symbolize the three stages in God's intervention in history, from the final one to the original one—namely, the Redemption, the Incarnation, and the Creation. Within each pair, as we will now see, one lens is much smaller than the other.

The pair of lenses closest to the Host, then, is the dogma of the Redemption. Christ redeemed mankind through His Passion and death on the Cross.

The second pair of lenses is the dogma of the Incarnation. God the Son, the Word Eternal, took flesh from the Blessed Virgin Mary and became man.

The last pair of lenses, farthest from the Host, is the dogma of the Creation. God created everything out of nothing, things visible and invisible. I will now describe each lens.

The Redemption

The first pair of lenses stands for the dogma of the Redemption. It combines two objects that, like the Eucharistic Host, are disc shaped (our "lenses"): the stone of Christ's sepulcher and one of Judas's silver coins.

Lens 1: The Stone

The first lens is the stone rolled against the access to the tomb of Christ after His burial. The stone of Christ's sepulcher shows victory over death. The dimensions of that lens are much wider than that of the Host, and its weight is enormous. "Joseph [of Arimathea] taking the body, wrapped it up in a clean linen cloth. And laid it in his own new monument, which he had hewed out in a rock. And he rolled a great stone to the door of the monument, and went his way" (Matt. 27:59-60). That heavy disc of stone expresses the power of death, a consequence of sin. Behind it, the dead body of Jesus of Nazareth was laid to rest. But the third day, "very early in the morning, the first day of the week, [the women] come to the sepulchre, the sun being now risen. And they said one to another: Who shall roll us back the stone from the door of the sepulchre? And looking, they saw the stone rolled back. For it was very great" (Mark 16:2-4).

That disc of stone was pushed away by God's power, as a sign of the Resurrection of Christ. "And behold there was a great earthquake. For an angel of the Lord descended from heaven, and coming, rolled back the stone, and sat upon it" (Matt. 28:2). Centuries earlier, to save Israel from the Philistines, David had thrown a stone into the face of Goliath, their giant champion. Satan, the father of death, was a much fiercer enemy than Goliath. But also, there was more than David on Mount Golgotha and at the nearby tomb. On the third day, as a sign of His rising, Jesus threw a much larger stone straight into the face of the devil, who fell vanquished. The Savior had washed that stone in the stream of His own blood, shed for our sins, and propelled it with the sling of His own flesh, lacerated for our redemption.

Besides their similar shapes, the Sacred Host at Holy Mass can evoke the stone of Jesus's sepulcher because the Host refers to Jesus as dead and contains Him as risen. When we look at the Sacred Host in the hands of the priest, we discern through faith the immense suffering endured by Jesus on our behalf and His glorious victory over sin, death and the devil at His Resurrection. All this is summarized in the stone of the sepulcher, rolled across the entrance and finally thrown aside. This is why the disc of stone is the first "lens" in the spectroscope of our Eucharistic enquiry. The spiritual component it identifies within the Host is victory over death.

Lens 2: The Coin

Judas's silver coin is our second lens. This disc is made of metal, not of stone. It is silver. It expresses the betrayal of Christ by any man through sin. "Then went one of the twelve, who was called Judas Iscariot, to the chief priests, And said to them: What will you give me, and I will deliver him unto you? But they appointed him thirty pieces of silver. And from thenceforth he sought opportunity to betray him" (Matt. 26:14–16). Christ died to save all men from sin. He did not need our assent to purchase the saving merits; but to apply them to our souls, He does. Whenever we reject God's grace, we betray the Lord. When we fail to respond to it with due generosity, to that extent we deny Christ.

Judas's regret is not true contrition. He still refuses to surrender to God's mercy. "Then Judas, who betrayed him, seeing that he was condemned, repenting himself, brought back the thirty pieces of silver to the chief priests and ancients, Saying: I have sinned in betraying innocent blood" (Matt.

27:3-4). As St. Peter explains, Judas's suicide is a desperate attempt to escape divine Mercy:

> Judas … was the leader of them that apprehended Jesus: Who was numbered with us, and had obtained part of this ministry. And he indeed hath possessed a field of the reward of iniquity, and being hanged, burst asunder in the midst: and all his bowels gushed out. And it became known to all the inhabitants of Jerusalem: so that the same field was called in their tongue, Haceldama, that is to say, The field of blood. (Acts 1:16-19)

The coin of silver expresses the price paid for our redemption — Christ's Precious Blood. But it is up to us to apply Christ's saving merits to the wounds of our soul, our sins. Such application is offered us chiefly when we attend with devotion the Holy Sacrifice of the Mass.

As we tried to discern the stone behind the Host, we may now discern the coin behind the stone. Despite their different sizes and material, both discs are intimately connected, like the scales of injustice to weigh the wages of sin. Notably, both are violently thrown back: the silver coins by Judas into the temple, and the stone by the angel after the Resurrection. This first pair of lenses exposes the wickedness of the perpetrators of the Passion and death of the Lord. It also manifests Christ's redeeming obedience and humility.

The Incarnation

The second pair of "lenses" in our dogmatic spectroscope concerns the Incarnation. These lenses are the apple in Our Lady's eye and the ovum in her womb.

A word of caution to our reader is needed about the vocabulary chosen to describe such a delicate topic. In Genesis 2:15, St. Jerome translates the Greek σπέρματος (spermatos) literally the "seed of the woman." By metonymy, the same word also means "posterity." The Fathers of the Church and the best theologians explain the Incarnation in very concrete terms. For instance, St. Thomas Aquinas asks "whether the Flesh of Christ was conceived of the Virgin's purest blood."[4] But their Latin original may sound as if lacking in discretion, once plainly translated into English. Through the eyes of such holy Doctors, we may learn to look at this most intimate—but decisive—part of God's plan with humility and purity, to better understand, revere, and give thanks. In that perspective, I hope that our use of the word *ovum* will be deemed acceptable.

Our Blessed Lady conceived the Son of God in her virginal womb after she accepted God's proposal in her immaculate soul. The biological event follows the spiritual one. Our Lady needed to say yes, or *fiat*, for the Word Eternal to take flesh from her. She first opened her eye to the divine light, assenting to God's holy will: "Behold the handmaid of the Lord; be it done to me according to thy word" (see Luke 1:38). Immediately after, God's power reached her womb, turning organic matter into a human being without having recourse to a man's seed.

Lens 3: The Apple

Thus, we need to contemplate these two spheres together, ovum and eye. The pupil of the eye, classically called "apple,"

---

[4] St. Thomas Aquinas, *Summa theologiae* III, q. 31, art. 5.

is a symbol of Our Lady's joyful and humble surrender to God. The New Eve offers that "apple" to the New Adam. He is pleased to accept it, repairing the sinful sharing of the first apple between our first parents. God enters through the eye of Our Lady's immaculate soul, unobstructed by sin, and takes flesh in her virginal womb. The will of Our Lady coincides perfectly with the will of God. The most secret recesses in her soul are infused with divine grace, just as, in her eye, the iris is dilated, painlessly, to welcome the One Who said: "I am the light of the world" (John 8:12).

Lens 4: The Ovum

At the moment when the Virgin consents, the original creation is renewed in grace, and its splendor is enhanced. Mary's womb becomes the firmament; God's people is revealed as the constellation; and the organic sphere journeying inside her, still of molecular size, is turned into the true sun of the world; the center of the cosmos of salvation.

Assuming a human body and soul, the Word Eternal begins to exist as Christ. God enters matter to reach our souls. In His Incarnation, God assumes to Himself organic matter (animated by a soul) for our Redemption. Thirty-three years later, on offering the First Mass the night He was betrayed, Christ gives His true Body and Blood as food and drink. The Holy Eucharist fulfills His abasement and His triumph of love.

When giving God full access to her soul through the wide-open apple of her eye, Mary conceived Love incarnate in her womb. Both shapes are aligned, ovum and apple, as twin lenses in our dogmatic spectroscope. They reveal to us the following truth as an essential component of the Eucharistic mystery: God became man as the New Adam to die for our sins and to feed us with His Flesh and Blood, received from the New Eve, Our Lady. The Holy Eucharist can be properly considered only in relation to the Incarnation, whereby, from the beginning, the Blessed Virgin Mary gave us her Son.

The Creation

The third pair of "lenses" refers to God's original initiative —namely, the Creation. It comprises two mineral spheres, the sun and the moon, which we take here as symbols of God's cosmic intervention. What is their relation to the Sacred Host, though?

When considering the Holy Eucharist, one should bear in mind that Christ, invisibly present under the externals of bread and wine, is the very same God who created everything out of nothing in the beginning. In the Creed during Holy Mass, a few minutes before the Consecration occurs, we profess God to be Creator "of heaven and earth, of all things visible and invisible." His power knows no limit.

He never acts arbitrarily, however. The rule of His creative power is His own sanctity, bounty, and mercy toward us. Supremely fulfilled as the Holy Trinity, God had no need to create in the first place. He did so for our sake, so that we may share in the joy of existing in His presence, manifested to us through the visible world.

The sun and the moon "praise" God (see Psalm 148) inasmuch as our human minds marvel at their splendor and beauty, as faint echoes of the perfections of their divine Maker. And yet, when the human race turned away from God through sin, it brought chaos into God's beautiful gift. Our sins disfigure God's creation when we cease to seek in His creatures the reflection of His magnificence.

Lens 5: The Sun

God made a new star appear at His birth in a stable, and He veiled another—our sun—at His death on the Cross. Celestial bodies are so obviously beyond human control that a change in their natural course is bound to impress men and secure their attention. This happened last at Fatima in 1917 with the miracle of the dance of the sun, witnessed by many thousands, including nonbelievers.

When we look at the Sacred Host elevated in the priest's hands, let us not forget God's absolute power over matter, regardless of quantity. If we find it hard to admit that God's human Body and Blood may dwell under the externals of bread and wine, let us remember that, for the Eternal Word, atoms are not essentially different from galaxies: both are matter in motion. His wisdom can combine them anew when beneficial to us, His beloved children.

Lens 6: The Moon

Not without a purpose, surely, did God make the moon four hundred times smaller than the sun, and also four hundred times closer to Earth. These balanced proportions provide us with the mysterious phenomenon of the eclipse, when a smaller body in the sky screens off a much larger one. Similarly, at the Elevation during Holy Mass, our eyes may witness an eclipse of the sun by what resembles a mere disc of bread.

Truly, the same God in the Host keeps in existence the distant sun and the moon. He once gave us the cosmos as a display of His love. But we failed to thank Him when His might was reflected in the stars. The same God is led by the same desire for our good when He now gives Himself to us as substantial Food. He has not changed. We have, when we fell from His grace. As a loving Father, God Almighty adapts His intervention to our new condition, as spectacularly as before, though no less tenderly. But the full moon, rising above the mountains or the sea, only *spoke of* God; while above our altars, the white disc of the Host *is* Him.

Alignment

Before I conclude this essay, let me draw an essential consequence from the stages just described. Sun and moon came first into existence—it was the Creation. Our Lady's apple and ovum appeared later—it was the Incarnation. The coin and the stone occurred at the end—it was the Redemption. These six objects were not manifested at the same time. And yet, in God's plan, they are simultaneous, because God is outside of time. In fact, the more essential certain things are to God's plan, the less they are subject to time, so that believers in every era can relate to them as co-present.

At Holy Mass, the white disc in the hands of the priest recapitulates the stages just described. But God's presence in the Host escapes our senses. It will save us in proportion with the intensity of our faith, animated by charity. Recalling in our memory these six round objects as lenses superimposed on the Host—as if all seven shapes were one—facilitates the assenting of our mind and heart to the saving truths symbolized by, behind the Host, the stone, the coin, the ovum, the apple, the moon, and the sun, respectively.

I would like now to show that there is more in this suggestion than a tip. Rather, aligning the seven circular shapes in our mind provides us with a vision of the combined stages of God's solicitude for mankind, from Creation to Communion. This helps us appreciate the intimate connection between the main mysteries of revelation. We realize better how, through this complex scheme, God reaches out directly to us, individually. Let me now offer an imaginary depiction of the Incarnation. What follows is no private revelation, but a meditation bringing together the dogmatic elements previously considered.

A Vision

Spring has just begun in Galilee. It is 3:00 p.m. in Nazareth. It is the eve of the Sabbath. Alone in her parents' house, a young girl is praying on her knees. She prays for Yahweh to deign to send the promised Redeemer, the saving Messiah. She knows of the creation of Adam and Eve; she knows of their Fall. She knows of God's original promise, that the seed of the woman will crush the head of the serpent. She laments the black tide of sin covering the earth, obscuring the sky.

At that moment, precisely, the light of day withdraws and darkness fills the room. Still upright on her knees, the maiden looks above through the light well in the ceiling, right above her. She has never before witnessed an eclipse. She watches the bright disc of the sun being gradually screened off by the smaller disc of the moon. She notices how the moon loses its radiance, turning to dark, as if disappearing, while its circumference radiates the brightness of the sun, shrunk to the size of our humble satellite. The maiden's face remains turned toward Heaven, but she closes her eyes to protect them from the radiation and because a Voice suddenly speaks to her soul.

Through the eyes of her soul, she sees the promised Redeemer. She sees His sufferings, His Passion and His death, as announced by the prophets. She hears that His mother is to share in all His torments, at least in her soul. Such is the condition of her becoming the mother, by her Son and through Him, of all men redeemed by the blood He will shed, the blood *she* will provide. She adopts them in Him, knowing at what great cost. In advance, she feeds them with His Flesh and His Blood, according to His will and that of His Father.

All Become One

On behalf of all men, she surrenders her soul and her body to God's adorable will. She says to the angel: "*Fiat mihi secundum verbum tuum* — Let it be done to me according to thy word." At that moment, she remembers the forbidden fruit, the apple in the hand of Eve of old, eclipsing the Face of God, as she presents it to Adam. She knows how the moon, right above her head, eclipses the sun despite it being 3:00 p.m., that Friday. All those stand aligned above her.

Below her, also aligned, but in the future, she sees the silver coins, the price of the Suffering Servant, the perfect Victim. She hears the stone rolling against the tomb of the Just. She believes in His final victory and, in advance, gives thanks — Eucharistically, for His flesh and blood offered for our lives. In spirit, she washes us with His blood and water and feeds us with His Flesh, since it is God's will.

What will connect this fateful past and this salutary future? What will turn the former into the latter? What will convert perdition into salvation? Now is the hour of the eclipse. Now is everything suspended. Now are all things aligned. Universal healing is just about to start.

Above the young girl's head, sun, moon, and (Eve's) apple float across space and time, aligned as one single disc. Beneath her tender knees, coin, stone, and Host await, prophetically aligned, as one disc and not three. She offers her apple to the pristine Adam. God receives her ovum and begins to be man.

In that instant, at that second, on the vertical axis of God's benevolence, sun, moon, apple, ovum, coin, stone, and Host meet at last; their lights unite; God's grace bursts forth; the night is gone. The eclipse is over, according to time. But it remains forever, according to grace. A maiden was kneeling. The Woman has risen. Our Mother walks across mountains and centuries, to visit her cousin, just become her daughter, and all of us her children dearly loved.

Conclusion

Through the light they emit, the chemical components of stars can be identified using the adequate tools. There is no need to travel to the star to gather samples of gases and stardust. From a distance, without physical contact needed at this first stage, human minds rest assured of what celestial bodies truly are.

Analogically, the Catholic Faith is the spiritual spectroscope offered to understand why it makes sense to say that the Holy Eucharist is God. Various "lenses" can be combined to analyze the doctrinal radiation emitted by the Sacred Host. I offered three pairs of lenses—that is, six circular objects aligned in God's saving plan for mankind. They are the stone of Christ's sepulcher and the coin of the betrayal; the virginal ovum and the New Eve's apple; and lastly, the moon and the sun. They are superimposed on the seventh "object"—that is, the whitish disc in the priest's hands that looks like bread but which God and His Church assure us is truly God.

No examination is more rewarding than this one. Beyond the "crust" of the Host, we learn to discern (1) the stone of

Christ's Resurrection and the metal of our sinful betrayal; (2) the true flesh of the Incarnation and the New Eve's apple—that is, her soul's perfect surrender to Light uncreated; (3) God's heavenly bodies propelled or obscured at will as compelling signs for men. At every Holy Mass, we may look at the Sacred Host in the hands of the priest as through a sextuple lens, our dogmatic spectroscope. This may help us find out what the mysterious Host is. The dogmatic light emanating from the Host is split into its component colors when contemplated through the six lenses—stone, coin, ovum, apple, moon, and sun—aligned in God's providential design.

Admittedly, more than our first eight months at seminary would be needed to explore such density of meaning. But even if only browsing through one's good catechism as a layperson in the world, how promising a journey for all!

Onward to Rome

At San Cristoforo Abbey, our Mass at dawn was now over. We remained a little longer to give thanks. Breakfast at the guesthouse did not take long, and, once aromatic Italian coffee and several panettones had pleasantly disappeared inside our young stomachs, we got into the cars. Over the hills of San Cristoforo, the sun was already high when we drove out of the abbey. We thanked God for the stellar light that accompanied us on our journey to Rome, to which all roads lead.

Our ancient Volvo had taken us across the Alps, and it could now climb the Tuscan hills! What chances were there, I thought, of a Swedish car carrying an American, a Pole, a Brazilian, a Lithuanian, and a few French and Germans across Swiss mountains toward the Italian capital? It all had a flavor of universality—another word for Catholicity. The Eucharistic "sun" was drawing every man and all things to Itself. Rome was its earthly see.

There, Sts. Peter and Paul, the two columns of the Church, had shed their blood for the love of Christ, followed by count-less others. There, thinkers and artists had displayed the truths of sacred revelation with such inspiration that even non-Catholics flocked to admire and give thanks. From there, despite all obstacles opposed by men's failures, the Eucharistic mystery radiated its warm light, enlightening minds and unifying souls. Spring was in the air.

3

The Transubstantiation

In the Church's Own Words

What is the meaning of *transubstantiation*?

Transubstantiation means the change of the whole substance of bread into the substance of the Body of Christ and of the whole substance of wine into the substance of His Blood. This change is brought about in the eucharistic prayer through the efficacy of the word of Christ and by the action of the Holy Spirit. However, the outward characteristics of bread and wine, that is the 'eucharistic species", remain unaltered.[5]

And because that Christ, our Redeemer, declared that which He offered under the species of bread to be truly His own body, therefore has it ever been a firm belief in the Church of God, and this holy Synod doth now declare it anew, that, by the consecration of the bread and of the wine, a conversion is made of the whole substance of the bread into the substance of the body of Christ our Lord, and of the whole substance of the

---

[5] *Compendium of the Catechism of the Catholic Church*, no. 283.

wine into the substance of His blood; which conversion is, by the holy Catholic Church, suitably and properly called Transubstantiation.

If any one denieth, that, in the sacrament of the most holy Eucharist, are contained truly, really, and substantially, the body and blood together with the soul and divinity of our Lord Jesus Christ, and consequently the whole Christ; but saith that He is only therein as in a sign, or in figure, or virtue; let him be anathema.[6]

If any one saith, that, in the sacred and holy sacrament of the Eucharist, the substance of the bread and wine remains conjointly with the body and blood of our Lord Jesus Christ, and denieth that wonderful and singular conversion of the whole substance of the bread into the Body, and of the whole substance of the wine into the Blood—the species only of the bread and wine remaining—which conversion indeed the Catholic Church most aptly calls Transubstantiation; let him be anathema.[7]

Fair Common Sense

How can billions of men and women believe that what their eyes see as bread is God? They are so many, of every walk of life, in every place and from every culture. They come from very diverse backgrounds. Some are rich, others poor. With more or less success, most of them strive for virtue, and many attain it. Among them are some of the greatest thinkers,

---

[6] Council of Trent (1551), Session 13, First Decree, chap. 4, quoted in CCC 1376 and in St. John Paul II, encyclical letter *Ecclesia de Eucharistia* (April 1, 2003), no. 15.

[7] Council of Trent, Session 13, Canons I and II.

poets, scientists, painters, architects, composers, scholars, politicians, and benefactors of humankind.

Let us refresh our memory with the following sample (purposely eclectic): Augustine of Hippo and Thomas Aquinas, the greatest thinkers of the first and second millennia; Leonardo da Vinci, type of the universal genius; Michelangelo, the painter of the Sistine Chapel; Galileo Galilei, father of modern science; Johannes Gutenberg, inventor of the printing press; W. Byrd, G. P. da Palestrina, W. A. Mozart, J. Haydn, and A. Vivaldi, best-known composers; Vasco da Gama and Christopher Columbus, explorers; John Henry Newman, an intellectual genius; Antoine Lavoisier and Louis Pasteur, fathers of modern chemistry and of bacteriology respectively; Oscar Wilde, a last-minute convert; Louis Braille, inventor of the reading and writing system for blind people; Eugenio Zolli, former chief rabbi of Rome; Claus von Stauffenberg, the German army officer who led the "Valkyrie" plot against Adolf Hitler; Takashi Nagai, a physician who survived the Nagasaki bombing and became an apostle of forgiveness; Dorothy Day, an American social activist; Alfred Hitchcock, the master of suspense; Grace Kelly, the Hollywood star turned princess; U.S. President J. F. Kennedy; Mother Teresa of Calcutta; S. Gutierrez, K. Chilton, and T. Jones, the first astronauts to receive Holy Communion in space; Rima Fakih, Miss USA 2010 and a convert from Islam; sportsmen such as American football quarterback Tom Brady, and Phil Mulryne, a former Manchester United midfielder ordained a Catholic priest; Shahbaz Bhatti, the assassinated federal minister for minorities affairs in Pakistan; J. R. R. Tolkien, a daily communicant—and countless others.

Could they all be complicit in an imposture on such a scale? No; they must be sincere. If not, how could such a lie be so well hidden, and for so long? It has been twenty-one centuries. It has spread all over the world. And even if they all pretended, to what purpose? What do they gain from it? Happiness? All men want happiness. If a sheer lie could secure happiness, why would not all embrace it, calling it "truth" for convenience's sake?

On the other hand, if they are sincere, those billions of fellow human beings, can they be sincerely mistaken? Are they all victims of an illusion? Are their minds so weak as to make a dream the touchstone of their existence? The Catholic Faith is a whole, whose every part must be believed and professed. But what they call the "Real Presence" of God under the externals of bread and wine is no minor part of their creed. On the contrary, it is its center and foundation. If that is false, everything else collapses. No wonder that, across the centuries, thousands of them gave up their lives rather than deny the Real Presence. Are they fanatics? No, since violence was inflicted upon them, not by them upon others. They meekly allowed their throats to be slit, while blessing God and praying for their torturers.

For want of a definitive answer, better leave them alone, those billions — alone with their belief. After all, if it makes them happy ... Other men and women have different convictions. Everyone is entitled to his opinion, as long as he doesn't impose it on others. Where all men see bread, including them, they believe God is present. They claim the same about wine. They can't prove either, of course. Or can they?

Which Two Kinds of People?

At first glance, there seem to be two kinds of people: those who think that what is real is only what they see and those who think reality is deeper than what they see. The first kind consider themselves scientific, or practical. The second kind are deemed the religious or artistic sort. But the divide lies elsewhere. Indeed, the scientific ones constantly rely on assertions they have not personally verified. This applies not only to algebraic equations such as $e = mc$ but to everyday life as well; for instance, they must trust that the taxi is taking them to their destination via the shortest route. As another example: those born after September 2001 have never seen the Twin Towers, except on television or in pictures, but they still believe in the past existence of the buildings. People in the other category, the religious and artistic sort, are by no means enemies to science and practical behavior. In fact, among them are the most realistic minds in the world. This point was humorously made by G. K. Chesterton with his Father Brown detective stories, in which the clerical sleuth uses common sense to unmask so-called seers and occultists.

Thus, to some extent, all men live according to what they see but also according to what they believe. Believing means to hold as real things we cannot see. Such things are not necessarily about religion. They belong to everyday life. A monk cannot see the love of God when praying before a shining icon, but neither can an agnostic *see* the love of his wife—he can only see her smile or hear her voice. Hopefully, he still holds as real that love that he cannot see.

For all men then, there is a surface, and there is a "below" or a "behind." And how could it not be the case, since our human mind is designed to abstract the essence of things from their appearances? Our five physical senses are like radar scanning the material world. Colors, sounds, smells, touches, and tastes reliably inform us about what things are "inside."

Stable characteristics such as round, green, smooth, and juicy allow us to identify an apple and not to mistake it for a leek. As such, even outside of religious considerations, we all relate to something "behind" appearances.

Let us now explain this truth philosophically.

Accidents and Substance

Humans are normally born with five sense organs: eyes, ears, nose, skin, and tongue. Those are the instruments of our five physical senses: sight, hearing, smell, touch, and taste. They are our natural radar to register what appears around us. Our five senses send information to our brains, which store it in our memory. With some experience, our brain learns to deduce what is behind from what appears. The range of our senses is limited. For instance, as we read these words, we can't see what our cat is doing in the kitchen, even less so in our neighbor's garden. Our senses are also limited in their spectrum, so that they fail to detect some phenomena occurring in our presence. For instance, we may see a dog darting past, and only later on, we may walk by its master holding an ultrasound whistle to his lips. The dog heard the whistle and we did not, because human ears cannot detect such signals.

Signals falling within the reach of our senses are called "accidents." The word "accident" here refers not to a car crash but to the downward movement of whatever falls (in), from the Latin *cadere*, "to fall." Such are the colors and shapes, the sounds, the smells, tactile sensations such as heat and cold, and finally the tastes, from mild to spicy, and from bitter to sweet. The accidents may change, without affecting what the thing is. For instance, a green apple may turn red without ceasing to be an apple. Four centuries before Jesus Christ, Greek philosopher Aristotle identified nine kinds of accidents: quantity, quality, relation, habitus, time, location, situation (or position), action, and passion ("being acted on"). In passing, let us observe that the Church has not invented the concepts of "substance" and "accident," like made-up tools to reach a predetermined conclusion. No, she borrowed them impartially from Greek philosophy.

The accidents express to us what a thing is. By definition, the accidents are what "falls" within the range of our senses, so that the thing itself, logically, is what stands below the surface, unreached by our senses. The Latin *sub-stare*, "to stand below" gave us the word "substance." Thus, the accidents are somehow the messengers or ambassadors of the substance to us. The accidents are less important than the substance. They may change while the substance remains—just as a king may change his ambassador without abdicating. On the contrary, if the king abdicates or dies, then his ambassadors lose their function. Whatever they may say cannot be on behalf of the sovereign anymore.

This point is very important. Accidental changes do not necessarily imply substantial changes. But a substantial change necessarily manifests itself through accidental changes. What appears on the surface may change while the inside remains. But the surface must be altered if what is under disappears.

Think of woodcarving, as an example. Wood is what the thing is. It may be carved first into a head and later on into a full human body, as for a crucifix. But such changes are accidental. They do not affect what the thing is, that is, wood. On the contrary, if the wood ceases to be wood—for instance, through burning—then its accidents will necessarily change as a result. Our senses will detect them as light flakes, greyish and dusty, heaped upon the floor: that is, ashes.

The same would apply to an ovum after fecundation. The ovum can undergo an accidental change such as its location, once released. But this change does not affect its substance. On the contrary, upon fecundation, the small organic entity produced by the mother acquires a new DNA, distinct from hers and from the father's. It is substantially modified, and this substantial change will be manifested through spectacular changes in the accidents, if nature is allowed to follow its course.

The Eucharistic Exception

As we have seen, accidents may change while the substance remains, but they cannot remain if the substance changes. The reason is that the accidents express the substance, being supported by it. They are the properties specific to the thing, as falling within the range of our five senses. If the thing changes, those properties will change as well.

The type of change occurring in the Holy Eucharist is an exception to this law of nature. In the Holy Eucharist, the accidents remain while the substance changes. In the ciborium, the Hosts still look like bread after the substance of bread has totally disappeared. Inside the Chalice, the liquid still looks like wine after the substance of wine has totally disappeared. This explanation was not given literally by the Lord Jesus or by His Apostles. The Holy Ghost revealed it to the Church as the rational articulation of the words of Jesus with the perception by our senses. Borrowing from a Greek pagan philosopher the distinction between substance and accidents, the Church believed that the Creator of the world changes the substance of bread and wine into the substance of His Body and Blood, even though the externals—or accidents—of bread and wine remain perceptible to our human senses.

In the Most Holy Eucharist, the change from bread and wine into the Body and Blood of Jesus occurs before our eyes, although undetected by our senses. In some rare occasions called Eucharistic miracles, Jesus has allowed those present to detect the change with their eyes. At Mass, it has happened that the priest and people saw the consecrated Host bleed (as in Bolsena) or become a piece of bloody flesh, and specifically of a human heart (as analysis showed in Lanciano). The priest and people did not communicate on those occasions. They were legitimately repelled by the prospect of cannibalism. Paradoxically, what surprises us as miracles in such instances is, in fact, the normal process of change, whereby the externals change *together with* the substances—those of bread and wine giving way to those of human flesh and blood.

Veiled, to Be Consumed

Since the Holy Eucharist is meant to be eaten by us, Jesus veils Himself under the appearances of bread and wine, that we may consume His true Body and Blood without disgust, but, on the contrary, with grateful decency. By virtue of His divine power, Jesus allows the externals, or accidents, of the bread and wine (perceived by our sight, smell, taste, touch, and hearing) to remain, even after their substance (that is, what truly makes bread, wine, or any object what it is) has been changed into the substance of His Body and Blood. So the accidents of bread and wine remain, while their substance vanishes, replaced by the substance of the Body and Blood of Jesus, present without their own accidents—or externals.

This is why, after the Consecration at Mass, the Host still looks and tastes like bread when in reality there is simply no bread left whatsoever, but only the appearances of bread veiling the true and real Body of Jesus. The same applies to the wine. One will not wonder how the body of a grown man can fit under the small dimensions of a disc of bread if one only remembers that the size is simply one of those external manifestations that may vary without affecting who a person really is—that is, his substance. Or else, was the Infant Jesus adored by the Wise Men and easily carried in His Mother's arms not the same Person whose grown-up body had to be stretched by several men nailing Him to the Cross?

So it happens with the Body of Jesus in the Holy Eucharist: the quantity of consecrated species in the ciborium and in the chalice is accidental. Whatever its dimensions, it is Jesus, truly, really, and substantially present, with His Body, Blood, Soul, and Divinity. Hence the tender precautions taken by Jesus' Mystical Bride, Holy Mother Church, for no tiny particle of Consecrated Host or any droplet of Precious Blood ever to be lost. As it is Jesus alive, under the appearance of Bread, the Host is not only Jesus' Body but also His Blood, Soul, and Divinity. For the same reason, under the appearance of wine, the Chalice contains not only Jesus' Precious Blood but also His Body, Soul, and Divinity.

Changing the Quantity of Food and the Quality of Drink

Jesus knew well that we find it hard to believe what we don't see. As a loving Teacher, He had prepared His disciples and us after them when He spectacularly demonstrated His divine power in relation to food and drink in particular: when He multiplied the loaves and fishes to feed thousands, and when He turned the water into wine at the wedding feast at Cana. In the first case, Jesus multiplied the quantity of food; in the second, He changed the quality of a liquid—turning water into wine.

From the very beginning, His Apostles believed in Jesus' Real Presence in the Most Holy Eucharist. With great insistence, St. Paul warns the first generation of Christians that "whosoever shall eat this bread, or drink the chalice of the Lord unworthily, shall be guilty of the body and of the blood of the Lord. But let a man prove himself: and so let him eat of that bread, and drink of the chalice. For he that eateth and drinketh unworthily, eateth and drinketh judgment to himself, not discerning the body of the Lord" (1 Cor. 11:27-29).

The successors of the Apostles, led by the successor of Peter, have always more deeply expounded this greatest of all the riches of the Church and have encouraged the Catholic faithful to draw the necessary spiritual sustenance from the transubstantiated Body and Blood of our Savior, who offers Himself to us in the Most Holy Sacrament of the Altar in a passionate embrace of faith.

Literally

Our Blessed Lord Jesus Christ spoke of Himself sometimes by comparisons, as when He said that He is the Vine and we are the branches; or when He said that He is the Gate and we are the sheep. But in the Most Holy Eucharist, He spoke not by comparison or symbol, but in a literal and true sense, saying that His Flesh is food indeed and His Blood is truly drink. The Jews understood it literally and were scandalized. Our Lord did not run after them to clarify a possible misunderstanding, although it would have been very easy for

Him to say that, as in other occasions, when He was speaking symbolically. On the contrary, He even challenged His Apostles about the literal understanding of His Eucharistic presence. But they trusted in His word, even though they admitted that they did not yet understand how they could eat His Flesh and drink His Blood. A condition to understand the Holy Eucharist is faith—faith in God's love for us and in His desire to take us to Him.

4

The Holy Eucharist as Judgment

"Judge me, O God!" To be judged? By God? Such is the petition frequently uttered by men in Holy Scripture. Why on earth do they beg to be judged? Don't they dread God's judgment? Initially, they want to be set apart from wicked and sinful men who possibly persecute them. In conscience, they find themselves blameless. Judgment thus considered is between the just and the sinners. It is to discriminate between "me" and "them": "Judge me, O God, and distinguish my cause from the nation that is not holy: deliver me from the unjust and deceitful man" (Ps. 42 [43]:1).

But in other instances, judgment applies to the individual considered exclusively, rather than in relation to others. Whereas the divide was between "him" and "them," it now gapes wide across his own soul. Within him, there is some good but also some evil. Life with God gradually leads the just to realize that he is not immaculate. He knows himself to be wanting to some extent, by God's standards: "If I would justify myself, my own mouth shall condemn me: if I would shew myself innocent, He shall prove me wicked" (Job 9:20). Only God is supremely holy and perfect—and by contrast, our most generous thoughts, words, and deeds are never totally immune from self-love, pride, and greed. As man becomes more aware of this discrepancy, he aspires to be judged.

This judgment is not expected to be a condemnation, though. If it were so, one would rather have it delayed until amendment could be offered, since no one wishes to be condemned, but saved. No, this judgment requested by the just is rather an assessment. He wants to know in what measure he pleases God. He wants to learn the truth about himself. By its very nature, our God-given intellect intrinsically craves the truth, so that even the reprobates would rejoice in knowing their sentence for the sheer certainty it provides — but since it implies the loss of God, their eternal End, damnation evidently casts any joy away.

This desire for truth applies to nonbelievers as well. Man has a craving for knowing. The greatest discoveries of explorers and scientists will never quench this thirst because they deal with matter and space (often for the benefit of mankind), whereas our souls seek truth and desire goodness. Identity does not come down to quantity, whether measured in light-years across galaxies or in atoms. We know that, ultimately, we cannot rely on the judgment of men, including our own, to reveal to us in certainty the truth of who we are.

Who am I? My name, my age, my sex, my fingerprints, and even my DNA don't suffice to define me, since they fail to provide a thorough account of the fulfillment of my soul. The truth about me should express how well or poorly I meet the expectations proper to my human nature, taking into account my particular skills and circumstances. What my boss may tell me about it, and my coach, my colleagues, even my parents, and my wife or husband — will never offer the perfect certainty I thirst for. And even if they laboriously could produce a figure assessing my present rate of existential fulfillment, it would be worthless an hour later, since I live in time, so my mood, my intentions, and my merits vary continuously. We thus long for a definitive pronouncement on our lives. A pronouncement that no further event will ever alter, once the heart in our breast has stopped beating. It can be granted only by a judge perfectly informed, unmistaken, prudent, uncorrupt, and, well, still alive after our soul separates from our body. This means God. Only God will judge us in full truth: "Judge me, O God!"

How Will God Judge Us?

Let us make a comparison. The places where men hide their greatest treasures, such as the Bank of England on Threadneedle Street in London or the United States Bullion Depository at Fort Knox in Kentucky, are protected by vault doors, altogether very heavy, thick, and equipped with highly sophisticated locking mechanisms. The thousands of components, including iron bars, wheels, springs, cables, and microchips could be compared to the millions of thoughts, words, and actions of a man's entire life. But only one code will set them all into combined motion, resulting in the opening of the door.

Imagine if such a door could think and feel! And imagine if that door knew it had never been opened yet! With what intent desire it would crave the finger that would type the unique sequence of letters and numbers! Then, and only then, would the purpose be met for which that door had been carefully designed, expensively purchased, and patiently assembled. It would open through a simultaneous activation of all its parts, following the typing of one word. Similarly, in an instant, without any mistake, God's judgment on our lives will reveal to us the truth about who we really are. It will identify the exact degree of our corresponding to His grace. It will pronounce on the fulfillment of our calling as human creatures to be redeemed by His mercy. That door of our life will open, then, either unto Hell or unto Heaven.

"He that despiseth me, and receiveth not my words, hath one that judgeth him; the word that I have spoken, the same shall judge him in the last day" (John 12:48). If a man has wasted the oil of divine grace, the assessment of his life will be like checking a machine that moves but does not breathe. His life summed up would translate into a number characterizing his specific wickedness, as a variation on the general character showing on the followers of the beast, as St. John teaches in his Apocalypse:

> And he shall make all, both little and great, rich and poor, freemen and bondmen, to have a character in their right hand, or on their foreheads. And that no man might buy or sell, but he that hath the character, or the name of the beast, or the number of his name. Here is wisdom. He that hath understanding, let him count the number of the beast. For it is the number of a man: and the number of him is six hundred sixty-six. (Apoc. [Rev.] 13:16–18)

Because by rejecting grace the wicked has forsaken the very life of his soul, by his own choice this man's judgment will be like scanning a barcode on purchased items at a supermarket. This soul sold itself to the devil. Mercy cannot read it.

We should do our utmost then, not to be found among the reprobates, but rather to be counted among the elect!

God's grace is offered to all, and His will is our salvation. How frequently, then, should we beseech Him, quoting again Psalm 42: "Judge me, O God!" How constantly should we pray to be judged favorably by Christ and to hear this intimate revelation promised to each of His followers: "To him that overcometh, I will give ... a white stone, and in the stone, a new name written, which no man knoweth, but he that receiveth it" (see Apoc. [Rev.] 2:17).

What is that mysterious "new name"? In the light of the comparison with the vault door offered above, we like to interpret this new name as the complex and unique "combination" disclosing the truth about each of our lives. That new name written is the instantaneous, concise, and comprehensive pronouncement on the lesser or greater generosity with which we will have corresponded to God's grace, offered to us in a diversity of ways during our life. With God's grace, our particular talents and circumstances destined us to collaborate for the redemption of the world. Hence, our naming will comprehend the specific weighing of our most secret thoughts, words, actions, and omissions—every whisper, every winking, every assent.

It will also consider our attenuating circumstances, such as our heredity, the wounds suffered in our past, our inhibitions and fears, our incurred disabilities and illnesses, our failed attempts. It will immediately identify the multiple factors combined to assess the exact imputability (i.e., moral responsibility) of all our actions; whether it was neglect, or pride, or ignorance or rashness or anger. Since those factors differ for every human being, God will not judge according to our external achievements or failures, but according to our deliberate will to collaborate with His grace.

To every elect then, a word will be spoken by the Judge—a word proper to them and used for no one else ever. Indeed, more than a word—rather, a name: our name of glory, freshly weighed out of the scales of God's love offered and received. That name will resound as the fulfillment of our baptismal name. The moment, indeed, when Holy Baptism was administered to us, either as infants or at the end of our catechumenate, was our formal beginning as adopted children of God. From then on, our entire life passed as a more or less faithful answering of God's calling. That "name of glory" is a name of deepest intimacy, because it has never been shared with, never been known by, never used for, any creature until us, and never will after. It belongs to no dictionary, having been composed by the justice and love of God as the exact expression of our unique identity.

As a comparison, a young poet in love will spur efforts to express in one stanza the uniqueness of his beloved, carefully choosing words and according sounds in exact reference to her outlook and her mind. Each verse in his poem could count as one syllable of a new single word, never yet printed or uttered. Even more so, our name of glory is the infallible assessment of the truth about us: the adequate expressing of our uniqueness by the Divine Word, who utters it to our heart as a nuptial gift on the threshold of eternal bliss. On hearing it, we discover for the very first time what we have meant to God during all those years spent on earth. And the revelation of such a love, which had accompanied us with such care amid all the difficulties of our life, causes us to wonder, to sob, to faint, and to melt in the embrace of the One whose grace configured us through faith, hope, and charity.

The following words addressed to God's people surely apply in retrospect to every faithful soul on receiving her name of glory:

> Fear not, for I have redeemed thee, and called thee by thy name: thou art mine. When thou shalt pass through the waters, I will be with thee, and the rivers shall not cover thee: when thou shalt walk in the fire, thou shalt not be burnt, and the flames shall not burn in thee: For I am the Lord thy God, the Holy One of Israel, thy Saviour: I have given Egypt for thy atonement, Ethiopia and Saba for thee. Since thou becamest honourable in my eyes, thou art glorious: I have loved thee, and I will give men for thee, and people for thy life. Fear not, for I am with thee. (Isa. 43:1–5)

Such is the judgment which the just beg of God. "Judge me, O God!" How high this judgment stands above any conception of earthly justice, however earnestly our best tribunals may try to reflect God's law! To be judged thus is at last to be known. It is to be fulfilled. It is to know the truth of who we are and to know that God grants this knowledge to us and that, as He shares it with us, He actually establishes us in the stability and permanence of our created perfection so that we will never disappoint Him. We further see that our worth gladdens Him; this, in turn, delights us. Oh, who would not want to be judged in that fashion? Who would not run to the Judge and entreat and plead to be tried and pronounced? When the judgment is life, and more than life—birth and fulfillment simultaneously, eternal gratitude and glorification! "Judge me, O God!"

There is more. Though our judgment will first occur individually right after death, it will be published at the judgment universal, applied at the end of time to God's entire creation. Which member of the Mystical Body of Christ, then, would not want his or her name of glory to be uttered after death, so that when time will be no more, the names of all the elect may be invoked in a simultaneous symphony of love—each name sounding as a syllable in the passionate name that the Savior will utter to His Bride: "Ecclesia!"

Confession and the Crucifixion

Let us recapitulate. We know that all men shall be judged by God when they die. We understand that they will be judged with perfect accuracy and fairness, and that the judgment will be unappealable, irreformable, and eternal. We believe that God wishes all men to be saved and that, for all, He provides abounding grace to fulfill their calling to holiness. If judgment is both unavoidable and crucial, then preparation is essential. Since Almighty God loves us perfectly, is it possible that He may lead us to our trial unaware or untrained? On the other hand, since judgment occurs after death, what anticipated experience can we have of it?

Our earthly trials and major steps can all be rehearsed to some extent. Students will take mock tests; would-be drivers will be instructed for hours across town; pilots will sit in flight simulators long before taking their first jet off the ground; dancers, actors, and singers will have dress rehearsals before the public can see their new show; even first-time expecting mothers will be told about the process of birth, with technical advice and explanatory pictures; and deacons will practice "dry Masses" for months before ascending the altar once ordained priests. In all such cases, the circumstances of the practice or test are designed to replicate as accurately as possible those of the actual event. Driving theory would not suffice to train the learner. He needs to sit at the wheel, in actual motion along the streets. Similarly, if a trainee pilot were allowed only to sit in a bumper car when a sophisticated flight simulator was available, he could legitimately think the training insufficient and could question the willingness of his instructor to have him pass the test. Also, merely attending the first Mass of a confrere would not properly train a deacon. He must spend hours at the altar, turning the right pages and holding the host in the correct manner, so as to be able to offer Mass worthily once ordained a priest.

What, then, of our training for entering eternity? Should we not rehearse judgment, so as to secure the best outcome when we die? If so, what circumstances will replicate those of our judgment in the most accurate way? Are we to spend days at the local tribunal to watch those being tried? Are we to take notes and memorize the most effective ways of inclining the judge in our favor? Are we to interview all those ever acquitted and learn from them any strategy? Are we to reenact our crimes as in a forensic reconstruction, surrounded by police officers, so that our active cooperation may dispose the judge in our favor?

Yes. This is just what God invites us to do. Yes, God invites us to attend judgment in a setting mercifully designed by Him as best suited to secure our eventual success. God calls us to expose ourselves to truth spontaneously now, so as to rejoice in it after we die. Let us now find out what this setting is. The *Catechism of the Catholic Church* teaches that in the Sacrament of Penance or Reconciliation,

> the sinner, placing himself before the merciful judgment of God, *anticipates* in a certain way *the judgment* to which he will be subjected at the end of his earthly

life. For it is now, in this life, that we are offered the choice between life and death, and it is only by the road of conversion that we can enter the Kingdom, from which one is excluded by grave sin (cf. 1 Cor. 5:11; Gal 5:19–21; Rev. 22:15). In converting to Christ through penance and faith, the sinner passes from death to life and "does not come into judgment" (John 5:24). (CCC 1470)

Thus, in this sacrament, Catholics conscious of having committed sins, will, from the age of reason, spontaneously present themselves before the priest seating as judge on behalf of Christ, with power to bind and to loose. On his judgment seat in the confessional, the confessor will normally wear the white surplice and a purple stole over his cassock, and possibly the biretta (not dissimilar to judges' head covers in many countries) to complete the vestmental expression of his judicial function.

According to the most ancient traditional idea, [this] sacrament is a kind of judicial action; but this takes place before a tribunal of mercy rather than of strict and rigorous justice, which is comparable to human tribunals only by analogy, namely, insofar as sinners reveal their sins and their condition as creatures subject to sin; they commit themselves to renouncing and combating sin; accept the punishment (sacramental penance) which the confessor imposes on them and receive absolution from him.[8]

---

[8] See St. John Paul II, apostolic exhortation *Reconciliatio et paenitentia* (December 2, 1984), no. 31.

As at a secular trial, charges are brought against a defendant—who is called here the *penitent*. The judge assures himself that all relevant evidences for or against the accusation are expressed. Weighing the attenuating or aggravating circumstances, he pronounces his judgment. The particularity is that the accused is not dragged into the box against his will, but rather, comes of his own volition and spontaneously makes the charges against his own person. He does so, by no means compelled by intimidation or against his good conscience, as at a Stalinian trial, but enlightened by the Spirit of truth and trusting in God's mercy. The comparatively lenient penance imposed would not by itself atone for the offense committed against God. An essential aspect of its purpose is to grant the sinner an opportunity to demonstrate his sorrow by collaborating, even in a small extent, to the restoring of the order and peace he has damaged. Healing, not condemnation, is the outcome. "Judge me, O God!"

Because of its judicial nature, the Sacrament of Penance, instituted by Christ, offers to every soul on earth a providential rehearsal for individual judgment after death. There is no doubt that a soul regularly exposed to God's healing truth through this sacrament is likely to be found after death in just the dispositions expected by God for admission into everlasting peace in Heaven. In fact, this sacrament not only anticipates an event to come; it also commemorates an event past. Soon after the beginning of human history, indeed, a trial took place, as described in the third chapter of the book of Genesis. God arraigns Adam and Eve, who had eaten the forbidden fruit, later hiding themselves. God prosecutes the case. He exposes the evidence. He gives the accused a fair chance to explain their conduct.

But they misuse this opportunity, blaming each other instead of confessing their guilt. God weighs the intentions and the circumstances and, in perfect justice, pronounces against Adam, against Eve, and against the serpent, adapting the sentence to the nature and responsibility of the three convicted. Lastly, the sentence is executed: Adam and Eve are expelled from the Garden of Eden, whose access is defended by a fiery angel. Those historical facts have consequences for human beings of any faith or none. Even nonbelievers experience an inner conflict between the good dictated by their conscience and the evil their will desires. All of us humans suffer from this essential contradiction because we have inherited human nature as wounded by the Original Sin of our first parents. In the Sacrament of Penance, God mercifully grants to each sinner a chance to confess and be reconciled with Him. From one sacramental absolution to the next, the soul grows in childlike familiarity with God, learning to love His justice and abide by it, not as a hindrance to her freedom but rather as her liberation.

As we have seen, Adam of old acted unjustly and, having been led into the presence of the divine Judge, was tried fairly and was justly condemned. But his sentence was mitigated by the promise of a Redeemer, i.e., Our Blessed Lord Jesus Christ, Son of the New Eve, Mary, and of God the Father. That New Adam always acted justly. But He was illegally arrested at Gethsemane, brutally questioned at the palace of the high priest, criminally tried by the Jews, and unjustly sentenced by Pilate to dreadful scourging and death on the Cross.

On Mount Golgotha

On Calvary, while hanging between the good thief, on His right, and the bad one, on His left, the New Adam acted by anticipation as supreme Judge, granting salvation to the one who repented. The arms of the Cross of Jesus literally represent those of the scales of divine justice, in whose pans the souls of all men will be weighed:

> And when they were come to the place which is called Calvary, they crucified Him there; and the robbers, one on the right hand, and the other on the left.... And one of those robbers who were hanged, blasphemed him, saying: If thou be Christ, save thyself and us. But the other answering, rebuked him, saying: Neither dost thou fear God, seeing thou art condemned under the same condemnation? And we indeed justly, for we receive the due reward of our deeds; but this man hath done no evil. And he said to Jesus: Lord, remember me when thou shalt come into thy kingdom. And Jesus said to him: Amen I say to thee, this day thou shalt be with me in paradise." (Luke 23:33, 39-43)

The bad thief refused to contrast his guilt with the innocence of Jesus. On the contrary the good thief, called Dismas, according to tradition, weighed the truth in his conscience against what appeared on Calvary. According to law and physical posture on the gibbet, Jesus was a criminal like him. But in his mind and heart, Dismas knew Jesus to be innocent whereas he was guilty, and he confessed his Savior's divinity despite His most contemptible situation as a convicted imposter and blasphemer nailed onto the wood, betrayed by His disciples, and abandoned nearly by all. Dismas discerned. Prompted by inner evidence, he pronounced against the externals. He let his reason and his conscience be guided by the Spirit of truth, lovingly trusting in God's justice and submitting himself to it in faith and hope.

Discerning and confessing saved Dismas. He pronounced against himself and for Christ, relying on no merit of his, but entirely on Christ's justice and mercy. Never was a rehearsal for judgment closer to the actual event. What an optimal preparation for the soul of Dismas, shortly to stand before the Redeemer after death, while his body still hung on the cross! For the practice and the actual trial took place in the physical presence of the same divine Judge, almost at the same instant and at the same place. And as he agonized, Dismas was canonized—by the Lord Himself: "This day thou shalt be with me in paradise" (Luke 23:43).

Hence, we may ask ourselves: What about *our* preparation? Are our training circumstances on earth less conducive to a successful judgment after death? We recall that the Sacrament of Penance truly sets us before the tribunal of God, in whose name the priest sitting in the confessional acts. And we give thanks for this merciful preparation to our ultimate trial after death. But do we not aspire also to stand in advance in the presence of our merciful Judge Himself, and not only of His priestly representative? Since it proved so successful for Dismas to anticipate his own judgment while breathing in Christ's real and physical presence, do we not wish we could confess directly to the Lord in our turn, like the thief, before we die? Emulating Dismas, could we not offer to Christ the loving homage of discerning and confessing His divinity, despite His external abasement? It would not be out of place. It would be truly human. It would not be a waste of time and energy. It would be most rewarding and salutary. Let us see how.

Guided by Christ's revelation as expounded for us by His Church, our intellect thus discerning would act according to its purpose, which is to seek the truth. God being the perfect truth, our intellect cannot act better on earth than when discerning His Real Presence. At the Last Judgment, Christ's presence will be obvious to all, making discernment unnecessary. When Christ comes with might and glory at the end of time, divine evidence will allow no examination. It will compel acknowledgment: whether lovingly by the just or hatefully by the wicked. Until then, could it be that discerning Christ's presence is our "main business" in this world? Could it be our very prerogative on earth? Furthermore, since our soul is not endowed with reason only, but also with willpower, God's presence once discerned must then be confessed through words and deeds. Our will thus confessing Christ's presence would act according to its purpose, which is to embrace the good. Training to confess God's presence is the best preparation for Judgment. Here below, Christ's presence is not evident, although certain. Applying to it the highest faculties of our souls, our intellects, and our will is our noblest and most salutary occupation. Reasonably discerning Christ's unobvious presence and humbly confessing it is our God-sent preparation for a favorable judgment. Only here on earth is it possible and meritorious.

We learn to discern and confess God's presence in the beauty of nature, in the virtues of our fellow men, in the privacy of our hearts when praying, and in the Church's means of sanctification. But nowhere has God granted us this opportunity better than in a sacrament, closely linked with that of Penance. In that other sacrament, God allows us to be in His presence, not only spiritual but real, true, and substantial. He does so as God-made-Man, Jesus Christ, through His genuine human Body and Blood, united to His human Soul and to His Divinity. What is this sacrament of paramount importance to prepare us for judgment? It is the Most Holy Sacrament of the Altar, the spousal gift of our Emmanuel to His Mystical Bride, the Church, and to each of her members: the divine and perfectly adorable Holy Eucharist. "O Sacrament most Holy, O Sacrament Divine, all praise and all thanksgiving be every moment Thine!"

The Most Holy Eucharist

Now that we have identified it, let us see how the Holy Eucharist prepares us for judgment. To that end, we simply need to recall to our memory all that we have already examined—namely, how men aspire to be told their moral truth; how this will occur at their trial by God after death; how God mercifully provides for them a preparation in this life; how the Sacrament of Penance is the closest judiciary rehearsal to judgment; how Dismas was saved *in extremis* after confessing Christ as the divine Savior, physically present; how this true presence is spread and offered to all nowhere better than in the Most Holy Eucharist.

After the Sign of the Cross (and the words '*In Nomine Patris*' etc.), the Eucharistic Sacrifice begins with the following quote from Psalm 42: "Judica me Deus—Judge me O God." Those words confess as sinful—and withdraw as shameful—the fatal claim of Adam and Eve to be judges of good and evil, as lured by the devil: "You shall be as Gods, knowing good and evil" (Gen. 3:5). Only God, Creator of all things, is perfectly good. Consequently, He only can tell in truth what pertains to goodness and what is alien to it; that is, what is evil. Angels and men merely learn from God to discern between good and evil. They do not fashion this distinction from their own insight or power. From the start, then, the Eucharistic Sacrifice strikes at the very root of all our problems—that is, the pride of creatures who foolishly believed they could supplant their Creator as supreme judges upon themselves and upon the world. We fell, because we claimed to discern good and evil independently from God.

What a powerful antidote then, when, right from the beginning of Holy Mass, all fallen children of Adam and Eve confess with contrition and gratitude that, far from being the authors of judgment, they are its objects: "Judge me, O God." We are not the judges; we are the accused, begging for mercy; begging for the truth about our individual moral fulfillment, which God alone can grant us. We throw away our usurped regalia, we leave our stolen seats of justice, and we prostrate on the ground before the only Judge: "Judge me, O God." Wonderfully, no sooner has our petition been uttered that we discern in our souls the dawn of truth, the balm of healing, and the warmth of peace. No slaves' words are those, but children's. We were lost, and we are found again: "Judge me, O God."

The same Ordinary of the Mass quotes Psalm 42 further: "Judica me, Deus, et discerne causam meam de gente non sancta: ab homine iniquo et doloso erue me"—"Judge me, O God, and discern my cause from that of a nation not holy; rescue me from a man unjust and deceitful" (see Ps. 42:1). That "unjust man" is not principally a distinct individual, but rather the "old man" within; the sinful part in every fallen human being. Through those words, the sinner exposes himself to God's truthful judgment, so as to be cleansed from whatever is sinful in him and to be confirmed in whatever is virtuous. This petition is the main theme of the Eucharistic Sacrifice, reiterated in many variations through the Kyrie, the Offertory, the Canon, and the Communion. What will be the divine response? How will God answer our desire to be judged by Him?

The divine pedagogy mercifully adapts to our nature by repeating the circumstances of our sin, so that, now humbled, we may learn from it and overcome the temptation. On Maundy Thursday, for example, after the arrest at Gethsemane, St. Peter denied Our Lord thrice, amid a group of people around the fire in the high priest's courtyard. Similarly, after His Resurrection, in an apparition by the lake, Our Lord will lead St. Peter to confess thrice his love for Him, as witnessed by the group of the Apostles gathered around the fire prepared by Jesus Himself: "Peter was grieved, because he had said to him the third time: Lovest thou me? And he said to him: Lord, thou knowest all things: thou knowest that I love thee" (John 21:17).

Long before that, Adam and Eve had willed to usurp judgment; to discern between good and evil autonomously, eating the forbidden fruit. In response, God leads us, their children, to make a judgment, also about a divinely appointed food. He asks us to discern His Real Presence in the Eucharist. It is God's merciful way to humble our original pride and to heal our natural faculty of judgment by applying it to the very sign of His love for us. It is as if He is telling us: "So, you meant to be judges in my stead? Well, my children, I take you to your word. Judge now of my love and pronounce on me. Will you confess that I love you enough to make myself present and edible, for the life of your souls, beyond the reach of your senses; or will you again set the finite range of your wisdom and bodily perception as the assessors of my mercy?"

What shall we answer? Of course our eyes see bread and wine. But Christ affirmed time and again that the Eucharistic species harbor His Body and Blood, not symbolically but literally. So does St. Paul affirm, as taught directly by the divine Master:

> Therefore whosoever shall eat this bread, or drink the chalice of the Lord unworthily, shall be guilty of the body and of the blood of the Lord. But let a man prove himself: and so let him eat of that bread, and drink of the chalice. For he that eateth and drinketh unworthily, eateth and drinketh judgment to himself, not discerning the body of the Lord. Therefore are there many infirm and weak among you, and many sleep. But if we would judge ourselves, we should not be judged. But whilst we are judged, we are chastised by the Lord, that we be not condemned with this world. (1 Cor. 11:27-32)

This teaching is of the utmost importance, being the only theological exposition in Holy Scripture on the Real Presence of Jesus in the Most Holy Eucharist. Significantly, it links presence to judgment. Discerning the presence determines salvation. The man who will discern the presence will escape condemnation. The man who fails to discern Christ's presence condemns himself. Here, discerning means to judge favorably. Our physical senses are summoned as witnesses to the Eucharistic judgment. They sincerely affirm that there is no Christ, but mere bread and wine. They are not mistaken. Only, they reach as far as their capacity allows, namely, to what appears externally. They are not deceived or lying; just limited—like a blind witness asked to testify about video footage; he would say that he sees nothing. Because we are spirits in a body, we naturally judge of the substance of any material being according to its external manifestations as perceived by our five senses—sight, sound, smell, touch, and taste. When we see a smooth, red, round fruit, for example, we conclude that it is an apple, not a pineapple.

In the Holy Eucharist, Christ invites us to realize that our senses, however useful, do not reach as deep as the substance of things. Ultimately, He calls us to trust more in what our spirit informed by faith understands than in the report of our senses, limited to externals. This is not to depreciate our senses but to exalt our spirit as a much higher component of our being. The same spirit, mainly composed of intellect, will, and memory, is confirmed in its nobler status and in its deeper outreach, when guided by Christ to embrace in reason and faith the reality of His presence, still hidden to our senses. It is explained elsewhere how the Eucharistic data, far from being unreasonable or arbitrary, opens the safest and most rewarding paths for human intellect in its search for objective truth. Our present examination limits itself to the Eucharist as judgment.

The Judgment of the Angels

Human beings are not the only ones whom God invited to reach out to Him beyond their immediate perception. Angels came first. God had created those pure spirits in a state of excellence that called for completion in closer union with Him. What specifically was the occasion or condition for the angelic fulfillment is not yet defined. A traditional hypothesis is that God revealed to the angels the mystery of His Incarnation. Those superior beings saw the second Person of the Blessed Trinity assuming our human nature. They would have understood the consequence of having to continue to adore Him not only as the uncreated Spirit, which He remained, but also as a man, which He would become. Such an abysmal abasement of the Godhead filled the good angels with loving awe. It revealed to them the unfathomable wisdom of their Creator, in whose sight they became forever established.

Other angels loathed the idea of having to worship God as united to humanity. They refused to bow their knee at the name of Jesus (see Phil. 2:10), considering it unworthy of their angelic nature. What they had perceived of the order of creation forbade such concealing of the Almighty Spirit under the lower form of a material being. They deemed the Incarnation unfitting for God and found their foreseen adoration of Christ humiliating. They were pure spirits like God and enjoyed that resemblance. God had not united Himself substantially with any angel, as far as we know, but by creating them, He had shared with them His own spiritual condition—although in a finite mode—and He destined them to an even closer union with Him. It was challenging enough that God would plan to extend this privilege to spirits of a lower order, the human ones, united to matter. But was it conceivable that mere human nature could be made divine in a strict sense, and adored? Was it admissible? Did it befit God's majesty, those angels objected—and their dignity? Denying it, many fell. They set themselves forever against God.

God had created all the angels out of love. They knew it and had justly felt honored. But to know truly God's bounty, they needed to be shown the gratuitousness of the immense gift of existence, of intellect, and of will that God had granted them. Up to that point, angels could think that, to some extent, they deserved God's munificence. By telling them His intention to share those precious gifts with creatures lower than them in dignity — that is, humans — God revealed to the angels that their glory was absolutely unmerited. For some angels, this discovery only opened their eyes to God's unfathomable generosity and transcendence. They gave thanks for this revelation of God's intimate nature and adored Him even more profoundly.

Other angels felt that this sharing of intellect and free will with creatures partly material was unbefitting. Those angels are like the resentful early workers in the parable of the laborers in the vineyard (Matt. 20:1-16). Having been created first (or called first, according to the parable), they can't accept that latecomers may receive the same wages — that is, a sharing in God's spiritual nature:

> And receiving it they murmured against the master of the house, saying: ... Thou hast made them equal to us. ... But he answering said to one of them: Friend, I do thee no wrong: didst thou not agree with me for a penny? Take what is thine, and go thy way: I will also give to this last even as to thee. Or, is it not lawful for me to do what I will? Is thy eye evil, because I am good? So shall the last be first, and the first last. For many are called, but few chosen.

Reading this parable in the context of the creation, one can almost hear God talking to the angels. Put to the test of divine condescension, some adore the Giver, while others scorn the gift. Their jealousy turns to hatred when they learn that the human race, which they despise, will not only be endowed with created intellect and will, but, in the case of the New Adam, will be made divine.

The call to humility, trust, and love that the Incarnation was to the angels, the Holy Eucharist is to men. We may look at matter as angels look at us. They are purely spiritual; we are spiritual and material; matter is not spiritual at all. Angels were glad to have been made sharers in the purely spiritual nature of God but were stunned by God's intention to unite Himself to a nature not purely spiritual, when becoming the man Jesus Christ. In our turn, we give thanks for our spirit and senses and for God's having become one of us. But we can't spontaneously accept that the God-Man could hide under the externals of mere matter—bread and wine—and expect us to adore Him in such abasement. And yet, this is precisely God's ultimate gift to us. Like of old for the angels, the prospect of God uniting His presence to a level of creation lower than us causes two opposite reactions among men: either of gratitude or of resentment.

First, why gratitude? Bread and wine obviously lack the intellect and will that make us superior. In the Holy Eucharist, though, God will come and appear as bread and wine. Intellect and will, then, are not necessary for God to abide in a created thing. This may come as a shock to us humans, if we thought that we had in any way deserved that God should become one of us. We realize that God ennobled and redeemed our human nature out of sheer gratuitousness. This truth is most convincingly professed through adoring Him in the Holy Eucharist, acknowledged as the true *manna,* the *viaticum* on our way to the Promised Land of blissful eternity.

Second reaction: Why resentment? God made us like Him when He endowed our race with intellect and free will. But men easily take the consequence for the cause. Instead of saying that God's gift to us of a spiritual nature reveals His generosity, they claim that it rather binds God to restoring His gift when it is damaged by our sins. God's intervention must aim at perfecting our mind rather than hindering it. Since our mind knows only through our physical senses, and since Christ's presence in the Eucharist escapes our senses, the Eucharist contradicts our human nature, so that it cannot possibly be true. To interpret literally the Eucharist is a misunderstanding, they think, clearly unworthy of God and of man.

Cunning and Humility

This is when clever people come up, apparently to offer a way forward when all seems blocked. One may thus imagine some angels exploring possible compromises with God's plan to become man. Some would allow God only to borrow the outlook of a man, as Archangel Raphael would later do when assisting young Tobias: "Then Tobias going forth, found a beautiful young man, standing girded, and as it were ready to walk. And not knowing that he was an angel of God, he saluted him, and said: From whence art thou, good young man?" (Tob. 5:5–6). Christ, then, would not have been truly a man, but like Archangel Raphael, he could have said: "I seemed indeed to eat and to drink with you: but I use an invisible meat and drink, which cannot be seen by men" (Tob. 12:19). Other angels would concede that a mere man, Christ, could be adopted by God later on, perhaps when baptized by St. John the Baptist in the Jordan. But the third option: Christ's humanity to be genuine, not apparent, and never to have existed separately from God the Son—such was a statement to which no angel could adhere without humbly stepping further into the mystery of God's almightiness and gratuitous love. Many did step forward.

Similarly, some men consider the Holy Eucharist to be mere bread and wine, only *symbolizing* God's presence. Others admit God's presence to be *loaded into* the bread and wine, turned into divine vehicles or containers during the liturgical gathering while retaining their material existence. But no man can embrace the Eucharistic truth—the true and literal conversion of the entire substance of the bread and wine into the substance of Christ's Body and Blood—without humbly stepping forward into the same mystery of God's almightiness and gratuitous love.

From the start, Christ did nothing to facilitate acceptance of this difficult doctrine. For example, explaining the process of transubstantiation would have helped His disciples, as it would have clearly ruled out any horrendous suggestion of cannibalism. Instead, Our Blessed Lord repeated several times in the most literal way the necessity of consuming His Sacred Body and His Precious Blood. He chose not to explain how this could occur with respect, beauty, and peace. While on Earth, Christ did not wish to impart a rational justification for the Holy Eucharist. That He would do later, through His Church.

The Lord's intention about the Holy Eucharist was essentially to call men to deeper trust and love, even challenging His Apostles.

The Jews therefore strove among themselves, saying: How can this man give us his flesh to eat? Then Jesus said to them: Amen, amen I say unto you: Except you eat the flesh of the Son of man, and drink his blood, you shall not have life in you. He that eateth my flesh, and drinketh my blood, hath everlasting life: and I will raise him up in the last day. For my flesh is meat indeed: and my blood is drink indeed. He that eateth my flesh, and drinketh my blood, abideth in me, and I in him. As the living Father hath sent me, and I live by the Father; so he that eateth me, the same also shall live by me.... Many therefore of his disciples, hearing it, said: This saying is hard, and who can hear it?... After this many of his disciples went back; and walked no more with him. Then Jesus said to the twelve: Will you also go away? And Simon Peter answered him: Lord, to whom shall we go? Thou hast the words of eternal life. And we have believed and have known, that thou art the Christ, the Son of God (John 6:53-58; 61; 67-70 [52-57; 60; 66-69]).

The virginal conception of Jesus, and even His divine identity, were hidden from the fallen angels. Satan tried to find out when he tempted Christ in the desert, but in vain. Some minor demons hatefully proclaimed the exceptional sanctity of the Christ. But without divine communication, no angelic spirit could know that this man walking in the dust, eating, sweating, and sleeping was God the Son. Human beings find themselves in a similar situation when looking at the Sacred Host. They see only bread and, left to their own capacities, they cannot say: "It is the Lord" (John 21:7). A leap in trust is necessary. We are called to pronounce on the reality of Christ's presence in the Holy Eucharist while we live, so that God may pronounce on the reality of His presence in our souls when we die. This obligation is not a test whereby God would cruelly force us to deny our human capacities. On the contrary, the Eucharist perfects our intellects and our wills by presenting to them as a single object the perfect truth and perfect good.

I said earlier that men crave to know the truth about who they are, and this will only occur when God judges us after death. We saw that God mercifully granted us preparation for our judgment, since He wills to find us innocent and immaculate, if only we collaborate with His grace while we live on Earth. The Holy Eucharist is the supreme preparation, designed by God Himself, to secure our favorable judgment. It takes place in time, as befits our human nature, whereas angels embraced or resisted God's plan immediately after having been created. When angels learned of God's Incarnation, it was not easier for them to reconcile it with His dignity and theirs as pure spirits than it is for us incarnate spirits when learning about the Holy Eucharist, whereby Christ makes Himself truly present under the externals of inanimate matter.

On both occasions, God's descent appears to angels and to men as a shocking abasement. Their only way to overcome their reluctance is to trust more radically in God, who will never act against His divine nature, nor against the angelic and human natures that He created out of love. The angels who followed God's plan were forever established in His grace and sight, while those who rejected it became demons. Men are similarly called to embrace God's saving plan. But the range and pace of our intellect are shorter and slower than that of the angels. For that reason, we may err and repent. Adapting His response to our weaker nature, God pedagogically enfolds the process of our redemption, whose summit is the Holy Eucharist. I called it our training for entering eternity. Before concluding, we now must examine how our Eucharistic preparation for judgment takes place.

Preparing for Our Judgment

Looking most reverently at the Holy Eucharist as our God-designed rehearsal for judgment, we should recall the context in which this sacrament occurs. It is called the Holy Sacrifice of the Mass. Holy Mass is the unbloody reenactment of the sacrificial death of Christ on the Cross, which merited salvation for all men. Holy Mass is meant to take place in a sacred building, designed and consecrated for that exclusive purpose. Earlier I asked whether we were to reenact our crimes as in a forensic reconstruction, surrounded by police officers, so that our active cooperation may dispose the judge in our favor. We answered positively. The liturgy of Holy Mass is such a reenactment, as I will now show.

Television series and films display very realistically the protocol applied in the tragic circumstances of a criminal investigation. The location is circumscribed with colored tape marked with the words "Crime scene—do not cross" repeated all along in capital letters. Onlookers must keep outside the perimeter. Trespassers are prosecuted, as they may interfere with the reenactment, willfully or not. Only those qualified by their training and mission may set foot within.

Analogically, a low wall or rail normally runs all across the church building, setting apart the sanctuary and the nave. The nave is the larger space where the congregation assembles. The sanctuary is the smaller area, equivalent to the crime scene, where only clergy are allowed. The accused and the witnesses may stand right outside the crime-scene tape, answering any questions asked by the officers. On rare occasions, they may be called within the perimeter. Just as police detectives and criminal investigators follow a set of pre-established rules, priests and sacred ministers in general abide by a set protocol of gestures and words regulating even what they wear and which utensils to use. This protocol is called the *rubrics*.

At the center of the crime scene, the outline of the dead body is marked across the surface whereupon it was found. This is obviously the most important area within the whole location. The outline delineates what immediately pertains to the victim, such as limbs and clothes. Similarly, at Holy Mass, the divine Victim is laid upon a square linen fabric called a *corporal*, spread in the middle of the altar. Nothing but the Victim must be placed within the perimeter of the corporal.

The event reenacted is the Passion and death of Jesus Christ on Calvary. Christ died to atone for the sins of every man. Every man then bears personal responsibility for the death of Christ. This is why all men are convoked as accused and convicted to attend this liturgical reenactment. The priest celebrant at Mass is the only one acting in the very Person of Christ, repeating the last words and actions of the Savior. But the priest is also a sinner, and, as such, he leads the people into confessing their guilt and begging God for mercy. When the divine Victim makes Himself truly present on the corporal under the externals of bread and wine, all those attending are given the perfect opportunity to confess that they have offended God, either directly or in the person of their neighbor, and to ask for forgiveness.

Holy Mass leads us into the dispositions of soul that must be ours at our judgment after death. But once our soul has separated from our body, it will have no power to change anything to its inner dispositions, for better or for worse. This is why our only chance is to make those dispositions habitual in us while we live. We would be very unwise to leave it to chance to inspire us with the adoration, thanksgiving, contrition, and supplication that God wishes to find in our soul at judgment. Securing those dispositions requires training, so that they should grow into habits and be our constant moral framework. This is never more fruitfully achieved than through Holy Mass, regularly and devoutly attended.

Only at Holy Mass are we granted the grace of talking to our Judge as physically present. During the Eucharistic Sacrifice, Christ is the One offering Himself to God the Father at the hands of the priest in atonement for our sins. He is simultaneously the Victim offered, the Sacrificer offering, and the Altar upon which the Sacrifice occurs. Christ is present at Holy Mass as dying on the Cross but also as gloriously rising, thus anticipating the resurrection of those His members who will have died in a state of grace. In advance, then, He is also the Judge of the living and the dead and will reward every good deed and vindicate every evil one at the universal judgment concluding history. Once well prepared through a good confession and sacramental absolution granted to us by the priest acting as the judge by proxy, we may walk into the church and, kneeling by the altar rail, present ourselves before Jesus Christ, at once our Brother, our Victim, our

Advocate, our Savior, our Judge, and our God. And we implore, "Judge me, O God."

Holy Mass refers back to the death of Christ on the Cross. But that latter event itself reenacted an earlier event: that of the Original Sin. As amply demonstrated by the Church Fathers, Christ, the New Adam, died upon the wood to expiate the first sin committed by the First Adam when he ate of the tree. The Original Sin took place in the Garden of Eden, and the Crucifixion also in a garden, as reported by eyewitness St. John: "Now there was in the place where he was crucified, a garden" (John 19:41). The Cross stands as a man-made tree, as opposed to the original tree of the knowledge of good and evil. The fallen pair of Dismas and Mary Magdalene, redeemed, represent Adam and Eve, our fallen parents; whereas the immaculate pair, Jesus and Our Lady, demonstrate the victory of God's grace over the curse of sin on behalf of mankind.

The evil spirit is most actively at work at the Crucifixion, as he was at the first temptation, but he is soon defeated through the obedience and humility of the New Adam. As explained earlier, Adam and Eve were tried by God shortly after their crime; while on Calvary, the unrepentant thief condemned himself, contrary to Dismas, who confessed, believed, and was saved. Sent away from Eden, Adam and Eve were expelled from the presence of God, until the New Adam would make God's presence real, true, and substantial in His humanity.

As Adam and Eve had eaten the fruit, the reenactment of Christ's Crucifixion entails the sharing of His Sacred Body and Precious Blood, as ordered by Him at the Last Supper on the very night He was betrayed. Eucharistic Communion completes our petition for mercy. When receiving our Victim and our Judge under the externals of bread and wine, we repeat the very crime of our first parents eating the forbidden fruit, the root and principle of our personal sins. We do so to our shame as convicts in our forensic reenactment, acknowledging full guilt; but also to our joy as children rejuvenated by God's forgiveness! In Holy Communion, we confess more eloquently than through any words, as we receive our Judge, that He is the divine Antidote to sin and death. Just before receiving Holy Communion, kneeling at the altar rail, thrice the communicant repeats: "Lord, I am not worthy that Thou shouldst enter under my roof; but only say the word and my soul shall be healed." "Only say the word"? What is that *word*? On trial before God, we await in total despondency to hear that word that His lips will utter. That word is God's verdict about us. As previously described, that word will take into account every thought, deed, and action as well as every circumstance in our life, and, instantaneously, it will manifest our lesser or greater corresponding to God's grace. Awaiting the speaking of that momentous word, we recall the much longer expectation of our human race as a whole, from the moment our first parents fell down to the manifestation of the very Word of God incarnate, Jesus our true Savior. Yes, in Holy Communion, the Word to be pronounced by God the Father is literally His only-begotten Son, our Emmanuel: "God with us." That word is not merely sounded as a vibration but is materialized under the externals of bread and wine. The Eucharistic Christ is our verdict.

In Holy Communion, Jesus, the cornerstone, is a touchstone, revealing our moral fulfillment. Such is our prayer, then, altogether contrite and blissful. We ask God-made-Man, Jesus Christ, our Victim and our Judge, to deign to come within us according to His will and make us now such as He wishes to find us at the hour of our death. Holy Communion is our judgment already enacted. When scorned or carelessly or unfaithfully received, it condemns us. When received in the right dispositions of humility and trust, it leads us into the open arms of the One whom we revere as our Judge and who embraces us as our Savior.

5

Gradation of the Modes of Presence

What Do We Mean by "Presence"?

According to our everyday experience, the word "presence" is used in many ways. Generally speaking, "presence" indicates that something, or someone, is somewhere. Thus, a music critic could mention the presence of nine singers on the stage, while a forensic doctor might note the presence of arsenic in a victim's body. Because things interact with each other, no presence is without consequence. A presence is either beneficial or detrimental. Uncertainty about the nature of a presence detected will naturally lead to concern or even fear. Violence may ensue as a means of preservation when a presence (of the unborn, for instance) is deemed invasive. For the modern agnostic (if we may briefly consider such a viewpoint) the ominous presence can be that of extraterrestrial, supernatural or bacteriological entities. Films depicting hostile presences, such as the *Alien* and *Resident Evil* film series, or *The Exorcist*, attracted vast audiences. These entertainments provide our technological age with a way of exorcising the fear embedded in a human race conscious of its vulnerability.

Societies deemed archaic or tribal by comparison with ours believed in invisible presences, whether of spirits or of demons, and learned to placate them and always feared them. Thank God, Christianity set mankind free, stating that the Holy Trinity, Christ, and the angels and saints are at work among us and that demons, our mortal enemies, are already defeated by Christ's Passion and Resurrection. Becoming aware of their presence is necessary for spiritual survival and fulfillment. Interaction with God and His intermediaries gives our lives on earth all their meaning, until we reach heaven, by God's grace. The heart of such interaction is the Most Holy Eucharist. In this "sun of all the sacraments," God-made-Man, Jesus Christ, is *present* to us in the fullest sense. To understand better how God is present in the Most Holy Eucharist, we need to explore the concept of presence as it encompasses many shades or degrees. This chapter does not aim to explain how the Eucharistic presence occurs (i.e., through transubstantiation) but simply to demonstrate why it is the deepest and most rewarding presence that man can encounter on earth.

The Man in the Street

Let us begin with the ordinary perception of the man in the street, regardless of his creed. In the Western world, at least, telecommunications, and the Internet in particular, have extended the concept of presence. "Where are you?" is the question most frequently heard in public transports and places, asked by mobile-phone users. At the other end, we are also made privy to the conversation when we hear the answer given: "I am on a train" or "I am at the hospital." People who know us and care about us mean to locate us if they are not physically present with us. When we chat with our friends on the other side of the planet, not only hearing their voices but also seeing their faces on the screen, it really feels as if we are in the same room. They are present to us and we to them. Anonymously, surveillance cameras provide a similar sensation of being in more than one place at a time. For example, a Londoner on a business trip to Germany can see on his smartphone the trash truck emptying the bin he left on the curb. Such modern presence is used far beyond the private sphere. Unnoticed by pedestrians and motorists, thousands of cameras inform traffic regulators and security agencies with live updating. In supermarkets, one can buy drones equipped with cameras to film not only one's own property, but also the neighbors' garden and—why not?—the inside of their houses. To prevent theft, many vehicles now carry a tracker that allows a control center to locate them at all times. Modern technologies have made the line between protection and intrusion thinner. This multipresence can make us feel dizzy.

A time comes when, after the excitement, we like to ask ourselves: "Where am I?" Fundamentally, we are in whatever place we focus upon; we are where we zoom in; we are where we think it matters to us. But are we always where we should be? Are we always where it benefits us? Are we always in a presence that fulfills us? To answer this, let us deepen our examination of the concept of presence, shifting now from our daily experience to the Holy Bible.

In the Beginning

"Where are you?" Such is the question God asked Adam immediately after the first sin. Its immediate implication is that Adam has withdrawn from God's presence. Indeed, the book of Genesis states: "When they heard the voice of the

Lord God walking in paradise at the afternoon air, Adam and his wife hid themselves from the face of the Lord God, amidst the trees of paradise. And the Lord God called Adam, and said to him: Where art thou?" (Gen. 3:8-9). Why does God ask Adam this question? Nothing is hidden from God. Everything lies open before His eyes. God knows not only material things, but even spiritual ones, such as our thoughts. Consequently, God knows very well where Adam and Eve are. He knows in which grove they hide and behind which trees.

Therefore, it is not for His sake that God asks, as if He needed the information. Rather, it is for the benefit of Adam and Eve. By asking, God helps our first parents realize that they have withdrawn from His presence. When breaking God's commandment, Adam and Eve have morally turned away from God. The physical distance they put between them and Him only expresses their moral estrangement. Their mind ignored God's law; their will despised God's love; their memory forgot that God had created them free, after His own image and likeness, and would hold them accountable for such a dignity. "Where are you?" is God's merciful and pedagogical way of telling Adam that something had just gone very wrong through his fault. "Where are you?" implies three things in particular: first, you are not with me anymore; second, you are the one who is lost; third, my asking is for your sake.

Before the Original Sin, Adam and Eve lived constantly in the presence of God. It was not something they felt physically, although God would not have excluded their bodies from the blessing of divine companionship. Being in God's presence meant a spiritual awareness of God and a desire for Him. Adam's and Eve's minds were always pondering the truth of God's law of life. Their wills always adhered to God as the perfect Good. Their souls were filled with God's grace, and their senses and limbs obeyed the sanctity of their souls. One can say that they bathed in God's holy presence. In the Votive Mass of Our Lady, the Church describes the Blessed Virgin Mary as "playing before God at all times, playing in the world" (see Prov. 8:30–31). The behavior of the New Eve would apply to the First Eve as well and to Adam before the Fall, as both were created without sin and had not lost the grace of God—yet. Thus, we can picture our First Parents "playing before God at all times, playing in the world." Later on, sin deprived them of God's presence. Their spiritual and physical faculties lost their orientation. They became fundamentally disoriented. They got lost. God's answer consisted in leading them back freely into His presence. He designed His plan of mankind's redemption as a restoration of the original harmony.

We could compare Adam and Eve after the sin, and the whole human race with them, to an orchestra rescued from a shipwrecked liner. Each instrument is carefully cleaned and mended, gradually tuned afresh, and finally played by expert hands to give its proper and full sound again. When the symphony reaches its climax, the sound is to all ears what God's presence is to men redeemed. God's breath and fatherly fingers produce in us vibrations of grace and unfold the harmony of virtues, to reveal and fulfill the perfection of our nature restored. The entire process of our salvation and sanctification consists in coming back into God's presence. Again, because both God and our souls are spiritual realities, such presence is not mainly physical. It is about our minds resting in God as the perfect Truth and our wills embracing God's as the supreme Good. Practically, how can this be achieved? Many created things are present to us; and we are present to many created things. But they can fulfill us only if they bring us closer to the Creator. Any presence benefits us inasmuch as it leads us back into God's presence. If the presence of anything created distracts us from God's presence, then we should ignore it.

Presence of Things and Presence of Persons

Let us make a first distinction between the presence of things and the presence of persons. I said that "presence," broadly understood, simply means the fact of being somewhere. In that sense, "presence" applies to inanimate things, such as stones; for example, the Crown Jewels are in the Tower of London. The term applies equally to rational beings; for example, the burglar is in the Tower of London. Because we are endowed with reason, presence is a richer concept when applied to rational beings. However, even about nonrational ones, such as minerals, plants, and animals, a preliminary question must be asked: Is the thing for real, or is it not? In other words, whatever makes a thing what it is, its substance, must truly be there for that thing to be present. Blank ammunition loaded in a movie gun is harmless; there is no bullet there. Tomato sauce spread on the actor's shirt is but tomato sauce; there is no blood there. The blast and smoke of the gunshot will be heard and smelled just as if a bullet had been fired; but none was fired. Also, the color and dripping of the tomato sauce will look just as if blood had been shed; but none was shed. Thus, even for physical things, presence should not be taken for granted, as externals can be deceptive.

Let us now consider presence in relation to persons. Persons are beings endowed with reason and free will, such as you and me and any human being. Persons also include Our Lady in

Heaven, angels and demons, and the three divine Persons: God the Father, God the Son, and God the Holy Ghost. Since we are human persons, the presence of other persons means more to us than that of nonrational beings, because there can be reciprocity of love and affection. This does not happen with our pets, much less with plants and minerals. Though our cat may seem affectionate or moody, it acts according to instinct, not knowing that it is a cat and that it could try to be a better cat. Only *persons* can be conscious of each other, that is, can interact at the level of intellect and free will. We can be present to a person, and that person to us. However, even persons are not present to each other always and in the same manner. Let us illustrate this point with a few examples.

A love letter is cherished and kissed as it makes one's beloved present in some way. If a picture or a keepsake is enclosed, the presence increases. Nowadays, videos and voice messages provide an even more realistic sense of the other's presence. Live video chats enhance it further. But total presence is reached only when the loved person can be heard and touched without any intermediary.

More than physical proximity, the intention of the other person also influences the quality of our mutual presence. When crammed inside a subway at rush hour, one wishes there were fewer persons present since, despite closeness, interaction is unrewarding. Everyone's intention is clearly to get to his destination and out onto the street as soon as possible. When reaching the pavement above, pedestrians are just unknown figures, whose lives remain separate from ours. We may walk close to one another, but indifference makes our presences mutually insignificant. Once at the parking lot, the uniformed attendant by my vehicle is certainly present and his intention is clear (to issue a parking ticket) but in opposition to mine (to get away with the infraction). Our encounter does not make me a much better person. If, then, after a hard day's work, I am awakened in the middle of the night by an intruder who has crept in through my window, whose torch swiftly locates my wallet and my smartphone and snatches both into his bag, he is very much present to me and I to him. But he does not act for my best interests, so that our shared presence certainly fails to enrich me.

Interacting with God

We have just seen some examples of interaction between human persons. Let us imagine some cases between God and us. At a basic level, God is present to us through the beauty of His creation. The order, the variety, and the harmony of the material world sing the praises of its Maker, for us humans to listen and learn about Him. Whatever exists, we may reflect, would collapse into nothingness if, for one second, God ceased to want it to be. Every morning we may thank God for His renewed gratuitous gift of life to us and to the world. If, instead, we misuse God's gift and expel God from our soul through mortal sin, we are still His creatures, still kept in existence by His generous almightiness. But what a deeper access to God's presence we have when Holy Baptism or sacramental absolution truly makes us temples of the Holy Trinity! Then God comes and dwells in us, to inspire and guide all our thoughts, words, and deeds according to His grace. Following the example of the saints, we learn to keep the presence of God. Whether we work or rest, cry or laugh, we try to do all things through Him, with Him, and in Him.

Based upon these considerations, we now reach the core of our reflection on the concept of presence. We first examined how modern technology extended the notion of presence among men, calling for discernment in its use. Going back to our origins, we then saw that our human race had been created in God's presence, where our first parents, Adam and Eve, enjoyed perfect felicity until they lost it through sin. From this, we deduced that our dealings with created beings should have one criterion—namely, how their presence leads us back into God's presence.

We first looked at nonrational beings and found that externals did not always suffice to indicate the true presence of a thing. We then considered the different ways human persons can be present to each other and concluded that bodily proximity is not enough. Rather, loving design is what fosters the most rewarding type of presence. Lastly, we described how God is present to us as the One providing existence, but even more intimately when welcomed as the Guest of our souls. It remains for us to see how a Person who is altogether man and God can be present to us and us to Him.

The Lord Jesus Christ is God the Son made man. He is true and perfect God and also true and perfect man. In Him, the divine and human natures are deeply united under one Person, who is God the Son. The Holy Name of Jesus means "Savior." But His second Holy Name, Emmanuel, means "God with us." Combining both Holy Names reveals that God saves us through living among us. Salvation is offered us through God's actual dwelling in our midst. Jesus spent thirty-three years living among us human beings. Among us, He ate, grew, yawned, slept, smiled, prayed, wept, suffered, and rejoiced. Before Jesus came, the Lord God dwelt spiritually in the Temple of Jerusalem, built as a shrine for the Ark of the Covenant, which had accompanied the Hebrew people on their way to the Promised Land. When the times were accomplished, Our Blessed Lady became the living Ark of the Covenant, when she carried in her virginal womb the true Son of God. Once born, Jesus manifested Himself to all men as the living Temple of God. His sacred humanity was the definitive shrine of the Godhead. His Body was truly God's Body; His eyes, lips, hands and heart truly God's as well as those of a man.

Countless people heard Jesus and were enlightened; touched His garment and were healed. Laying His hands upon hundreds, He cured them according to their faith. He even brought several back to life at their families' requests. Later on, nearly all forsook Him. But for the salvation of all, He suffered His Passion, died on the Cross, and rose again the third day, founding His Church. No religion ever imagined that God could make Himself so close to fallen and suffering men. Jesus took upon Himself our sins and planted the divinity in our nature. No salvation is granted to men but in the Lord Jesus. We need only to come to Jesus, to look at Jesus, to touch Jesus, and we are saved.

But how can we do this, since He is not visible on Earth any longer? We cannot find Him in the Temple at Jerusalem, since it has been destroyed, as He prophesied. We cannot meet Him in any bloody sacrifices, as they are not His own.

How the Lord Jesus Is Present

We long for His presence, but not only a spiritual presence offered us when we pray. Because we have a body, we need to be reached by God according to our nature, that of incarnate

spirits whose souls can receive nothing but through the intermediary of their five physical senses. Jesus is *Emmanuel*.
He saves us through His true presence in our midst. Let us
review the various modes of His saving presence.

First, a low level of the presence of Jesus is achieved through
the inspired depictions of His beautiful countenance in so
many icons, mosaics, paintings, and sculptures. Looking with
devotion at those artworks (even simple or naïve ones, provided
they are reverent) brings us in close spiritual contact with the
Lord they represent.

Second, when we endeavor to serve Jesus in His vulnerable and suffering members, the unborn, the poor, the sick,
the imprisoned, the lonely, it is He whom we reach, as He
assured us: "As long as you did it to one of these my least
brethren, you did it to me" (Matt. 25:40).

Third, when we pray with those gathered in His name,
we know that He is there, in our midst. So the very ancient
Christian hymn "Ubi Caritas" attests. Possibly dating from the
time of the Apostles, it bears witness to the spiritual presence
of the Lord among His children: "Where charity and love are,
God is there. Christ's love has gathered us into one. Let us
rejoice and be pleased in Him. Let us fear, and let us love the
living God. And may we love each other with a sincere heart."

Fourthly, Christ is present to us in a more physical way
in the relics of His saints, imbued with the grace of God.
Jesus inspired the saints during their lives, and they died with
His love burning in their souls. While on earth, they were
living members of Christ's Mystical Body, the Church. Soon
enough, on Judgment Day, their bones will be reunited with
their blessed souls, and their sacred bodies will be restored
to radiant integrity. When we kiss their remains, we confess

Christ's love and power. This is why, several times during Holy Mass, the priest celebrant kisses the altar stone in which relics are sealed.

Fifth, in God's Holy Word proclaimed, it is again Jesus whom we encounter. At a solemn high Mass in particular, the Gospel preparation and procession unfolds as a liturgy of its own, centered upon Christ's Word. The deacon will receive the book of the Gospel, possibly enshrined in a precious silvery case, glittering with gems. He will lay it upon the altar while assisting the celebrant in imposing incense. He will then kneel with the sacred book in his hands, receiving the priest's blessing to proclaim the Good News of salvation: "May the Lord be in your heart and on your lips that you may worthily and fittingly proclaim His Holy Gospel. In the name of the Father, and of the Son, and of the Holy Ghost. Amen."

When ordained, the new deacon would have heard the bishop say: "Receive the power to read the Gospel in the Church of God, for the living as well as for the dead; in the name of the Lord." Those formulas emphasize the cultural scope of the liturgical singing of the Gospel at Mass. The primary end of this sacred action is the worship of God, and its effects reach not only the souls of those standing in the nave but even of those lying in the grave. As Our Lord came into the world, died, and visited the souls of the just in Limbo before His Resurrection, the Gospel ceremony could be termed an Incarnation in sounds. Let us watch it at length.

The Gospel procession, with master of ceremony, incense- and candle-bearers, deacon, and subdeacon now stands still, facing north. The deacon, having bowed low before the sacred Book, incenses it three times, bowing low again afterward.

He then announces the title and signs the Book and himself three times upon his brow, lips, and heart to sanctify his thoughts, words, and affections. Then the very words uttered by God are proclaimed in Latin, the sacred language of the Church, following the ancient Gregorian melodies hallowed by centuries of humble and anonymous inspiration.

The sound vibrations travel from the mouth of the sacred minister across the sanctuary and nave, meet the frescoes on the walls and the stained-glass windows, and reverberate into the eardrums of the faithful, later to reach their souls and sanctify their lives. It is Christ who makes Himself present through those sacramental melodies. The book of Gospels is carried to the celebrant for veneration, held by the subdeacon, who omits the mandatory genuflection as he walks in front of the tabernacle: a telling expression of the pride of place held by the proclaiming of the Gospel at Holy Mass, which, in this instance, takes precedence even over the Eucharistic presence reserved at the altar. No Protestant liturgy comes near to showing to the written Word of God the reverence that Christ's Bride, the Church, paid it, long before the Augustinian Fr. Martin Luther would voice his claim of *sola Scriptura*, or "by Scripture alone."

The Gospel liturgy prepares us for something even greater. In the Old Testament, God trained His people over centuries through His patriarchs and prophets, whom He commanded to speak His words of conversion and faith. This was to prepare His people to welcome the unfathomable mystery of God's Incarnation in Jesus Christ. Similarly, the solemn proclamation of the readings, and especially the Gospel during Holy Mass, is meant to prepare the congregation for an event of greater import. This event occurs after the

Offertory, during what is called the Canon of the Mass. It is the Consecration: when God the Son, made Man, Jesus Christ, makes Himself present truly, really and substantially under the externals of bread and wine, with His Body, Blood, Soul, and Divinity.

The Eucharistic Presence

Recalling to our memory the various ways of being present we have examined, let us see how the Eucharistic presence of Christ includes and surpasses them. Externals can be deceptive, and so they are in the Holy Eucharist. In it, the true Blood of the Lord is shed, albeit invisibly, as the result of the genuine Sacrifice of Calvary made present anew at Holy Mass. Despite their outward characteristics of bread and wine, the Sacred Host and the liquid in the Chalice are not *things*, however sacred — they are Jesus Himself. His Eucharistic presence puts us in contact with the whole world created by Him and recapitulated in Him, who is "the Alpha and the Omega" (Rev. 22:13). It unites us with all the living and the dead — alive in God — who believe in Christ and do His Father's will.

The presence of Jesus in the Holy Eucharist is not that of a man indifferent to us, like some anonymous pedestrian, as the two disheartened pilgrims to Emmaus found out when Jesus broke the bread at the inn (Luke 24:30–31). In the Sacred Host, Jesus does not intrude in our lives like a burglar eager to evade our vigilance and take our possessions away from us. Admittedly, at the end of time He will come by surprise: "Wherefore be you also ready, because at what hour you know not the Son of man will come" (Matt. 24:44). Meanwhile, His true presence in the Holy Eucharist is our best preparation to meet with Him successfully at the end.

Christ's presence in the Eucharist is most powerful because He is there in Person, permanently, and not as a transient grace, as in the six other sacraments. The sacraments are the Church's most precious treasures, because in them Christ Himself acts for real. When a priest says: "I baptize you" or "I absolve you," it is Christ who truly acts through His minister. But in the Holy Eucharist Christ not only acts, but also dwells and remains, to be talked to and to interact with us without interruption, as long as the externals of bread and wine remain. As St. Pope Paul VI taught: "This presence is called 'real' not to exclude the idea that the others are 'real' too, but rather to indicate presence par excellence, because it is substantial and through it Christ becomes present whole and entire, God and man."[9]

In the Holy Eucharist, the Lord Jesus lovingly focuses on each one of us as if each of us were the only one in the world. Never distracted, bored, or tired, our divine Savior awaits us in the tabernacle of our local Catholic church to bestow upon us the graces our circumstances require. The more we reciprocate His attention, the more we are fulfilled. This encounter occurs through faith. Sensations are irrelevant. Faith teaches us that His presence is not merely spiritual and symbolic, but actual and physical, as He is there alive with His true human Body and all that pertains to His human nature.

Lastly and most importantly, the Eucharistic presence is supreme because Christ is in the Host and Chalice as sacrificed for our sins and also as resurrected for our salvation. As

---

[9] St. Paul VI, encyclical *Mysterium Fidei* (September 3, 1965), no. 39.

a consequence, it is the adorable will of Christ that we should receive Him in Holy Communion, expressing that no other good than Him, the Lamb of God, can feed us and keep us unto life everlasting. To that end, we must be absolved in Confession from any grave sin, and lovingly surrender our lives to Him, our Redeemer. His presence embraces ours then, as He literally dwells in us until our stomach digests the sacred Host (within about fifteen minutes after receiving Communion). During that time, we are closer to Him than we ever will be to another person; and through Him, we are mystically united with all those who seek and serve Him.

Since Our Lord's Ascension into Heaven and until His Second Coming in glory, nowhere on Earth is the presence of Jesus greater than under the Sacred Species in the Most Holy Sacrament of the Altar. A consecrated Host does not merely contain Jesus; it does not simply refer to Jesus; it does not symbolize Jesus—no, it *is* Jesus. There is no way offered to us men by which God our Creator and Redeemer is more present than in the Blessed Sacrament of the Eucharist, both during the Holy Sacrifice of the Mass from the moment of Consecration and outside of Mass in the tabernacle or in the monstrance.

That supreme mode of presence of Jesus in the consecrated Host and Chalice thus deserves acknowledgment, care, and honors spectacularly greater than toward any lower and less perfect modes of His presence in the world, in things and in men. The more we meditate upon this Catholic dogma, the less time we will wish to spend away from this divine radiation. The Most Holy Eucharist will appear to us for what it is truly: "God with us." In such presence, we will wish to spend our days, until we see God face-to-face.

6

Who Says "Hocus Pocus"?

Homily given by Fr. Armand de Malleray, FSSP, at the First Solemn Mass of Fr. James Mawdsley, FSSP, at St Mary's Shrine Church in Warrington on July 10, 2016.

"Say but the word!" Let the *new* priest say the word. Let *him* speak to us. Why this custom at First Masses to have another priest give the homily? After all, the one we came to hear is the newly ordained priest. It is Fr. James Mawdsley we want to hear. Let *him* speak to us words of wisdom. We want to know about his life. We want to hear about his adventurous journey, from a Burmese jail to a Bavarian cell; from prison to seminary and beyond. Let him "say but the word," and we will rejoice.

Dear friends, you are right. Like you, I yearn to hear our dear newly ordained priest speak to us (with a genuine Lancastrian accent). But did you know that, traditionally, even newly elected popes would not speak to the crowd on their first appearance on the balcony of St. Peter's Basilica? Would they just stare in silence at the jubilant flock then? No. They would say but the following words, all in Latin: "Sit nomen Domini benedictum" – "Blessed be the Name of the Lord.

Our help is in the Name of Lord. May Almighty God bless you, Father, Son and Holy Ghost." And that was all. No speech, no wishes? Nothing sensational? No program for the pontificate? Not a clue for the Vaticanists?

Just the opposite, in fact. God's blessing to men, imparted by God's priests, is *the* fundamental program. When you think of it, those words are the most important ones. They are the ones we most need to hear from the Vicar of Christ and from a newly ordained priest. What words? Jesus is Lord. God blesses us. No priest matters alone. Christ matters. The word we truly need to hear from the priest is Christ Himself, since Christ is the eternal Word of the Father. If a priest does not speak the Word Incarnate to us, that priest will not save us. If a priest speaks about himself, instead of Christ, his words are wasted. His words are sinful because he was ordained for one thing: to speak Christ to us. To communicate the Savior through his words to our souls. Speak then, dear priest, speak to us: "Say but the word!"

Have patience, dear friends: Fr Mawdsley will soon turn to you and speak to you. Before Holy Communion, he will present to you the Divine Victim, white and immaculate in his hand, and he will proclaim: "Ecce Agnus Dei, ecce qui tollit peccata mundi!" — "Behold the Lamb of God, behold Him who takes away the sins of the world." And you will unite with the server answering, talking to Christ Himself: "Say but the word, and my soul shall be healed."

We Desire a Healing Word

"Say but the word!" We desire a healing word. We need a word to travel to us. We want a word to be sent to us, to touch our ears and, through them, to resonate in our souls and to cleanse our hearts. We need this saving Word, because our souls are wounded, because our hearts are deaf. Indeed, our souls cannot hear. They will not listen. Why such an infirmity? Why?

Remember: when Adam and Eve turned away from God, when they committed the first sin, they shut themselves up against God's love. They stopped listening to the voice of God. That divine voice had created the entire world, but they ignored it. That divine voice had uttered words of spectacular splendor and of loving might:

> Be light made. And light was made.... Let the dry land appear. And it was so done.... Let the earth bring forth the green herb.... And it was so done. God also said: Let the waters bring forth the creeping creature having life, and the fowl that may fly over the earth under the firmament of heaven.... Let us make man to our image and likeness: and let him have dominion over the fishes of the sea, and the fowls of the air, and the beasts, and the whole earth, and every creeping creature that moveth upon the earth. And God created man to his own image. (Gen. 1:3, 9, 12, 20; 26-27)

Rather than listen to God's beautiful voice, to God's generous law, Adam and Eve believed another voice. Whose voice? The voice of the devil, luring them: "You shall not die.... You shall be as Gods" (Gen. 3:4-5). As a result, their souls lost interest in the nourishing Word of God. They ceased to welcome the life-giving Word of God.

"Say but the word, and my soul shall be healed." But God sent His Word into our world, into our flesh, to save Adam and Eve and all of us, their fallen children. Our healing is through hearing anew the saving Word of God. We are like victims after a bomb set off by terrorists. The blast of the explosion has damaged our inner ears. We need healing so that we may hear again. We need the Word that saves. We need the only Sound that can reach wounded ears and restore hearing to our souls.

Who Will Speak That Word for Us?

And *who* will speak it for us? Who will say but the word of life, that we may be healed? Will our parliaments and tribunals say but the word of life, that justice be done? Will our schools and universities say but the word of life, that truth may be taught? Will our media say but the word of life, that we may be informed? Will our entertainers say but the word of life, to recreate our souls? Will our pharmacies and hospitals say but the word of life, that we may be cured? Will they? Do they? They should. They could. Few of them do it, though. If only all of them were docile! If only they all loved light and served life! Meanwhile, and until judgment, *who* will say but the word, that we may find peace and forever rejoice? I ask you. Who?

The priest. The priest is the one who will say but the word of life — no other word. The priest is the one empowered to speak Christ to us. But how can he do that, you wonder? Will seven years of seminary suffice for him to say but the word of salvation? How many doctorates are needed to speak Christ? How much eloquence? And is Fr. Mawdsley not too young? Are they not *all* too young: should not one have lived several lives to speak Christ to us relevantly?

You are right, dear friends. Your priests could have all that, ideally, but it will not suffice. Spiritual formation, diligent studying, and human experience are needed, but only as means to an end. What end? The priest must not only speak to us *about* Christ. Any professor can do it, any historian of religion or sociologist can. Rather, the priest must essentially speak to us Christ Himself. Literally. What do I mean by literally speaking Christ? I mean this: "Take and eat ye all of this. For this is my Body." Again, what do I mean by literally speaking Christ? I mean this: "This is the Chalice of my Blood, of the New and Eternal Testament: the Mystery of Faith: which shall be shed for you and for many unto the remission of sins."

This is "speaking Christ" to men and women, literally. This is what the priest—and only the priest—is empowered by God to perform. When the priest speaks those most sacred words during Holy Mass, it is Christ who speaks through him. It is Christ who makes Himself present: truly present, really present, substantially present under the externals of bread and wine. Such is the Word, the saving Word, that the priest is called to speak. He speaks it every day. He speaks it at every Mass. He speaks it for the greater glory of God the Father and for the salvation of souls.

What the Devil Says

Pardon? What did you say? Someone just spoke. Somebody just spoke words: not words of life, though. I hear his voice. Can't you hear it? This voice murmurs close to our ears. Listen ... "Hocus pocus. It is all some silly magic." This voice suggests that such a change of bread and wine into God Incarnate is not true—that it *cannot* be true, that it *must* not be true. This voice suggests that we come down to earth—and forget Heaven! This voice asks us to be *reasonable*, to be *scientific*.

This voice demands that we should leave superstition behind and should stand up as adults for the honor of mankind! This voice proclaims that we cannot allow the Eucharistic claim: "Before Consecration the host is round, white, light," it says. "So it remains after Consecration: round, white, light. So it remains inside: just bread and nothing more. There is no change inside, if the outside remains. Transubstantiation is a dream, a sham, a lie. No," the voice goes on, "if there be a God, He is in the Host perhaps *symbolically*, not literally."

My friends, what will we answer the prince of this world —that fallen angel? Will we keep silent? Will we be impressed? Will he shake our faith? God forbid! Rather, we will answer this: that there is a God and that he knows it too well, he who forsook Him. We will unmask him, the father of lies. He denies the power of priests to transubstantiate bread and wine into Christ's true Body and Blood, literally. Why, then, in the desert once did he ask the Sovereign High Priest to change stones into bread? Did he doubt the power of the Word Incarnate then? In fact, the devil knows full well the truth of this Eucharistic change. He knows that Jesus truly takes the place of the bread and wine, while their externals remain.

As with utter reverence we swallow the Sacred Host, the devil envies this sweet and divine *possession* that Love grants to our souls, and he wishes hatred could match it. The devil believes in transubstantiation, and he trembles. He wants to possess our souls with hatred, and the Host prevents him from doing so. Mad with terror and with jealousy, his usual trick is to claim for himself the very power he cannot defeat. That is why he boasts of transubstantiating. He affirms, in his turn, that externals remain while inside substances are swapped. Every day he transubstantiates. Every night he transubstantiates. Everywhere he transubstantiates. How does he do it? We can't ignore it, tragically.

Consider. The priests of God take bread and they say but the word: "This is my Body"—and bread is no more, and Jesus is there. Such is our *faith*. In contrast, the prince of darkness takes tiny babies and says to the world: "This is *nobody*." Such is his "science." The externals remain: the limbs and tiny fingernails, the gestures and smiles go on just the same as before, and in the tiny chest, the heart continues to beat. But inside, we are told, a radical change occurred. Before a contrary law was passed, the mother carried a human person in her womb, her baby—but once the dreadful words are spoken to her, by her, only organic matter, only living matter, is now to be found. This is magic!

Faking Transubstantiation

Some reject the Holy Eucharist as unscientific because no molecular change can be detected after transubstantiation: the DNA is still that of wheat (as if a microscope could show the substance). And yet, they detect no change either in the DNA of a fetus, at whichever stage of gestation, before or after any law is passed about him or her. Its DNA is still *not* that of the mother, nor that of a strawberry, but of a distinct human person. It was never the same as the mother's and never will be. "Never mind, Baby's gone!" *science* and *law* proclaim.

Such is that alleged transubstantiation. "This is *no* baby. This is *nobody*. This is *your* body. This is *my* body." Every time such incantations are spoken by a parliament, by a tribunal, by a physician; even by a lover or, worse, by parents: "This is nobody—this is just something," the devil's transubstantiation occurs. Just like a miracle. Instantaneously, Baby ceases to be Baby; he becomes living matter, disposable at will. How many men and women are thus enthralled by this legal magic? None is unscathed. Some are mere victims. How many are misled into saying: "This is *my* body"? We know that many speak those words under pressure, out of ignorance or because all other paths seem blocked. God only knows their hearts: *we* must pray for more light.

Of course, the devil *lies*, fooling many souls in the name of freedom. He fakes the power of the living Word. He speaks but one word, "Death," and innocent human lives are turned into gold by Banned Personhood (name altered) and other so-called reproductive health providers, more successful than the alchemists of old. Instead, the priests of God speak but the word, and mere matter — bread and wine — is turned into life, human life, divine life: Christ, Life Itself. Dear Friends, I ask you today, during this First Mass of our dear new priest: Whom will we believe? Whom will we follow? Who will give us life? Whose flesh will feed us: that of our children — or that of the Lamb?

Born to Feed Us

As if we did not know ... As if we had forgotten that the Prince of Peace, Jesus, chose to be born of a woman, in a town whose name, Bethlehem, means "House of Bread." As if we had not seen Him lying as Food in a manger. As if we had not noticed that this posture of Christ as our heavenly Food, far from being accidental, is the very sign given us by the angel: "And this shall be a sign unto you. You shall find the infant wrapped in swaddling clothes, and laid in a manger" (Luke 2:12).

As if we could ignore that King Herod, inspired by the devil, tried to snatch from us our heavenly Bread, when he "killed all the [male] children that were in Bethlehem, and in all the borders thereof, from two years old and under" (Matt. 2:16). As if we had forgotten that the Savior inaugurated His public life at Cana by turning water into wine, later to change wine into His Blood. As if we did not see that He subsequently multiplied bread twice to feed His people, later to give His own Flesh as the Bread of Heaven.

"Say but the word!" The Word of Life. Yes, my friends, God in His mercy has empowered men with His divine prerogative over His creation. God, in His mercy for us fallen children of Adam and Eve, calls men from among us, such as Fr. Mawdsley, to make Him really present in our midst. God-made-man, Jesus Christ, in His mercy makes Himself truly present — not symbolically — under the externals of bread, in the most Holy Eucharist. Let us give thanks for such a wondrous Gift! Let us rejoice, for a new priest is given to us. Soon at the altar, for us he will say the Word. For us he will utter: "This is my Body" — and God will be there, living and saving in our very midst.

Conclusion

I conclude with the one who gave us Jesus. She is Our Lady. She is our Mother, the Most Holy Virgin Mary, the Immaculate Mother of God. This place is hers. This beautiful church in particular is St. *Mary's* Church. We want to be hers as well. We want her to lead us to Jesus, since she is the shortest way, the safest way, the only way to Him. Please note that she is not a priest. And yet, before any priest ever said the word, she spoke, at the Annunciation. When she responded to

Archangel Gabriel: "Fiat—let it be done," at that moment, by the power of God, what was so far only organic matter in her virginal womb was made a human child (and divine): Christ, the Word made flesh. And God dwelt among us.

Oh, sweet Mother of the High Priest, teach us to love your Son! Mother of priests, obtain for us thousands of holy priests! Our Mother through grace, say but the word, and our country shall be healed. Say but the word, and England (or any reader's fatherland) shall be thine again. Say but the word, and our land shall be cleansed from its iniquity. My friends, listen. She is about to answer. What will she say? She will not say "This is *nobody*"—since she is the Woman who crushed the head of the serpent. She will not say "This is *my* Body" because she is not Christ but His Mother. She looks at England; she looks at the hearts of all of us sinners, contrite and hopeful. She sees every man, every woman and child, and she opens her lips, saying but these words: "This is my *Dowry*."

7

Eleison! The Latin Mass in One Greek Word

The Most Holy Eucharist occurs at Holy Mass. The Holy Sacrifice of the Mass is the liturgical setting in which the Savior first gave His Flesh and Blood to take away the sins of the world, mercifully. The Year of Mercy declared by Pope Francis ended on November 20, 2016. But the petition for divine mercy will go on within the Church until the Last Judgment. As an enduring witness, it is enshrined in the traditional Roman Missal, the very same one that St. Faustina, St. Padre Pio of Pietrelcina, and so many saints used daily and that confirmed the aspirations of their souls. This essay shows how the traditional Roman Missal used by a growing number of devout Christians worldwide is all about divine mercy, as one of its prayers states:

> O God, Your almighty power is made most evident in Your mercy and pity. Be even more merciful toward us, that we may aspire after Your promises and come to share Your heavenly rewards. Through our Lord Jesus Christ Thy Son ...[10]

[10] Collect of the Tenth Sunday after Pentecost.

"Lord, have mercy!" We are so used to this petition repeated at every Holy Mass, that we may not realize how essential it is. "Lord, have *mercy* – Kyrie, eleison!" The retention
of the original Greek words even in Masses offered in other
languages shows how old this prayer is, rooted in the worship
of the very first Christian communities. Holy Mass is all about
mercy. No wonder, then, that the word "mercy" occurs up
to twenty-two times in the Extraordinary Form Missal, from
the Vidi Aquam to the Leonine Prayers. St. Thomas Aquinas
defines mercy as "the compassion in our hearts for another
person's misery, a compassion which drives us to do what
we can to help him."[11] Mercy can be shown by God without
altering His perfect happiness, as He removes the cause of
our unhappiness: sin.

At Holy Mass then, we sinners, penitents, fallen children
of Adam and Eve, are encouraged to ask God for mercy. We
ask for mercy because we recognize that we have sinned and
we know that God wishes to forgive us. The more we understand that God is good, the more we wish to be reconciled
with Him. This implies that our sins be taken away from us
as an effect of God's mercy. "God acts mercifully, not indeed
by going against His justice, but by doing something more
than justice."[12] This is why the Eternal Word became flesh in
Jesus Christ and suffered His Passion: to take away the sins
of the world, that we may have life eternal. This was achieved
through Our Lord's Passion and death on the Cross. Since
Holy Mass is the unbloody reenactment of Christ's unique
Sacrifice, nearly every prayer in the Missal involves mercy,

[11] *Summa theologiae* II-II, q. 30, art. 1.
[12] *Summa theologiae* I, q. 21, art. 3.

as we shall now see. For the sake of brevity, we will skip synonyms and consider only the instances where the word "mercy" itself appears.

Sprinkling Mercy

"*Asperges me, Domine*—Thou shalt sprinkle me O Lord." On Sunday, in preparation for Holy Mass, the celebrant sprinkles holy water over the congregation. It is a rite of spiritual purification. Those droplets of water should be considered as having journeyed across space from Golgotha and across time since the year 33, as St. John witnessed: "One of the soldiers with a spear opened his side, and immediately there came out blood and water" (John 19:34). From the start, we worshippers find ourselves in spirit at the foot of the Cross; not to mourn but to expose ourselves willingly and hopefully to the saving power of the Lord's Sacrifice. Holy water comes first, reaching our skins—the Precious Blood will follow, entering our mouths. From the start, we ask for mercy: "Miserere mei, Deus, secundum magnam misericordiam tuam"—"Have mercy on me, O God, according to thy great mercy."

One may think that this supplication would end with Lent, once the penitential season is over and the Church focuses joyfully on her Savior's triumph. How telling, then, that from Easter onward, in Paschaltide, the same rite of sprinkling (then called Vidi Aquam) still points to mercy, no longer sought but now secured, and thus a cause for thanksgiving: "Give praise to the Lord, for He is good: for His *mercy* endureth forever." Before Easter as well as after, the congregation asks further: "Show us, Lord, Thy *mercy*."

When the celebrant reaches the foot of the altar, he confesses his sins and asks the congregation to intercede for his forgiveness, to which they reply — or the server on their behalf: "May almighty God be *merciful* to thee, and forgiving thy sins, bring thee to everlasting life." In return, after the faithful have confessed their sins, the celebrant intercedes for them: "May almighty God be *merciful* to you, and forgiving your sins, bring you to everlasting life." He adds on behalf of all: "May the almighty and *merciful* Lord grant us pardon, absolution, and remission of our sins." Then follows a dialogue whereby God is requested to be favorable. The celebrant asks anew: "Show us, O Lord, Thy *mercy*."

Reaching the Altar of God

Once he has ascended the altar, the celebrant alternates the Kyrie with the server. It is the emblematic petition for divine mercy, a real summary of Holy Mass. A triple invocation is addressed to each of the three divine Persons, since none within the Blessed Trinity ever acts separately. Nine times, then, the walls of the church reverberate the humble, passionate, and hopeful "Eleison — Have *mercy!*" To God the Father: "Lord, have *mercy*. Lord, have *mercy*. Lord, have *mercy*." To God the Son: "Christ, have *mercy*. Christ, have *mercy*. Christ, have *mercy*." To God the Holy Ghost: "Lord, have *mercy*. Lord, have *mercy*. Lord, have *mercy*." From a literary perspective, one could say that this prayer is rather poor. By contrast, other prayers of the Missal are masterpieces of creative balance and theological concision. Not so with the Kyrie. There is no time. There is no need. By then, those present know too well what their most urgent necessity is: the removal of their sins. They are also well assured of God's willingness to grant it through His mercy. Both convictions meet in the plain repetitions addressed to the divine Persons. Their lack of style betrays the humility that inspires them, the urgency of our need, and the assurance of an answer.

With the Gloria, it would seem that the penitential mode is over. God's mercy is now secured. We progress with confidence toward its sacramental outpouring in the Consecration and Communion. The mood is one of jubilant praise, as the very words of the angels on Christmas night are now quoted by human tongue: "Glory to God in the highest, and on earth peace to men of good will." And yet how striking when, in the midst of such exultation, again mercy is asked for: "Who takest away the sins of the world, have *mercy* on us." Truly, the sinners' petition for mercy is not somber or gloomy after all. If it can occur in such a happy context, it shows that the consciousness of one's shortcomings does not weigh down those who trust in God's bounty. On the contrary, it fosters rejoicing, as the Church dares to proclaim during the Paschal Vigil in the Exsultet, describing the Original Sin: "O happy fault that earned for us so great, so glorious a Redeemer."

The Gloria insists then: "Who sittest at the right hand of the Father, have *mercy* on us." At this stage, we realize that divine mercy is one side of the same truth whose other side is human sinfulness. The more we acknowledge the latter, the more we benefit from the former. Neither can be handled separately. Focusing on God's mercy without understanding it as a response to the calamity of sin will sterilize its healing power. Reciprocally, clinging to our sins in shame like Judas, instead of throwing them into the furnace of God's mercy like Peter, will drag us down into Hell. God showed mercy when creating us, but even more when redeeming us.

In preparation for the Gospel, the celebrant prays the Munda Cor, begging God thus: "Vouchsafe, through Thy gracious *mercy*, so to purify me, that I may worthily announce Thy holy Gospel." His sinfulness makes him unworthy, he knows, of acting as God's herald. But he confesses that the Good News he is mandated to proclaim includes his own salvation and that of the human race. Even as an ordained minister, he knows that his service is acceptable to God not by virtue of personal merit, but as a consequence of God's mercy, which cleansed him.

Nearing the Sacrifice

The Offertory emphasizes the sacrificial destination of the bread and wine, rather than their human origin. At the Consecration, they will become the Sacred Body and the Precious Blood of God-made-man, Jesus Christ. The need of an exchange between man and God is not ignored, though. This appears at the incensing of the bread and wine: "May this incense blessed by Thee arise before Thee, O Lord, and may Thy *mercy* come down upon us." While speaking these words, as the rubrics instruct, the celebrant "incenses the gifts, thrice swinging the thurible over the Chalice and Host together in the sign of the cross, and thrice around the Chalice and Host, that is, twice from right to left, and once from left to right." The aromatic smoke of the incense ascends over the bread and wine as an expression of mankind's humble and trusting prayer. In response, God's mercy is expected to descend upon the altar. Such is the exchange. But how telling that our petition be uttered while the sign of our redemption — the holy Cross — is made three times with the thurible over the matter that will become the Savior.

Similarly, during the Canon of the Mass, God's mercy will not descend anywhere on the altar, or directly to sinners, but straight upon the bread and wine as they turn into the Redeemer. Again we see that the avowal of our sinfulness is the key to open the treasures of God's infinite mercies, poured upon us through His Son, confessed as Savior, adored as God, and welcomed as our Life in Holy Communion. Even the graces of spiritual Communion stem from the Eucharistic presence, mercifully.

Washing his fingers, the celebrant recites the second half of Psalm 25. Verse 11 states: "I have walked in my innocence: redeem me, and have *mercy* on me." The celebrant stresses that his justice is not his own. It does not express merits of his. The only reason he is innocent, unlike the "men of blood," is that God's mercy has either cleansed him from any grave sins or prevented him from committing them. This confirms the fact that mercy is not slavishly wanted but is filially hoped for. Acknowledging one's frailty and even one's sins is not meant to lead to despair or merely to a bleak outlook on life, but rather to excite humility and prudence because of our weakness, and confidence in a loving and fatherly God.

The word "mercy" occurs only once in the Canon of the Mass. Such scarcity, however, does not indicate a diminution of mercy. On the contrary, mercy is brought to its climax through the words of Consecration, whereby the Savior Jesus Christ, offers Himself in sacrifice to the Father on behalf of all sinners. Only after this, however, is mercy expressly mentioned. This occurs after the intercession for the deceased. Having requested that God may allow them into His presence in Paradise, the celebrant now includes the living in this petition: "To us also, Thy sinful servants, who put our trust in the multitude of Thy *mercies*, vouchsafe to grant some part and fellowship with Thy Holy Apostles and Martyrs."

After the Our Father, the celebrant develops its last petition, that is, to be delivered from all evil. He asks this through the intercession of the saints, adding: "Grant us peace in our days, that through the bounteous help of Thy *mercy*, we may be always free from sin and safe from all disquiet." Speaking on behalf of the congregation and of the whole Church, the celebrant stresses anew the radical incapability of men to fulfill God's holy will unless succored by divine grace. Far from any pessimism, this further statement is healthy realism prompted by love, based on the Lord's statement: "But to whom less is forgiven, he loveth less" (Luke 7:47).

The Lamb of God

Holy Mass can be compared to Mount Golgotha. We pray the Kyrie on our way up; reaching the summit, we witness the Consecration-Crucifixion; and at the same distance on our way down, we find the Agnus Dei. Like the Kyrie, the Agnus Dei is a triple invocation to God. But since we are after the Consecration, Jesus the Word Eternal is now physically present on the altar under the externals of bread and wine. Consequently, the triple petition is addressed directly to God the Son made man, the only Victim perfectly acceptable to God: "Lamb of God, who takest away the sins of the world ..."

Since Our Lord's Passion, no bloody sacrifices are valid or licit anymore. We don't see animals slaughtered on the altars of the true religion. For that reason, the word "lamb" may have lost its sacrificial meaning for us. Instead, it may spontaneously evoke cute woolly creatures frolicking across flowery fields; perhaps with ribbons tied around their necks as at Trianon, Queen Marie-Antoinette's made-up farm in Versailles. If the Lamb of God takes away the sins of the world, though, it is because He suffered His Passion as the perfect Victim, covered with His own Precious Blood. Our confidence stems from the infinite power of His human and divine Blood, shed for our sins. By the virtue of His Blood, then, we dare to beg of Him twice: "Have *mercy* on us!" The third petition to the Lamb of God states the deliverance from all suffering through peace bestowed.

Toward the end of Holy Mass, before the celebrant imparts the Last Blessing, he prays for his offering of Christ's Sacrifice to bear fruit: "Through Thy *mercy* may it bring forgiveness to me and to all for whom I have offered it." Again we see that God's mercy is the condition for forgiveness to be granted to men. Having nearly reached the end of the sacred action, the celebrant knows that through his offering in the very Person of the Savior of men, mercy is being poured upon souls, including his own.

Thanksgiving Prayers

Customarily, a few prayers are said after low Mass. Added for historical reasons, they can also be used in general for thanksgiving. The Hail, Holy Queen teaches us to salute Our Lady as "Mother of *mercy*." Since Mary is the Mother of Jesus, Jesus therefore *is* mercy. What a beautiful way of referring to the Savior, using the very word "mercy" as His first name. Divine mercy stems from the Most Holy Trinity; it is embodied and merited by Christ and most efficaciously petitioned by His Immaculate Mother. We thus beg Our Lady: "Turn then, most gracious advocate, thine eyes of *mercy* toward us."

Adding two more occurrences of the word mercy, the prayer following the Salve expresses this: "O God, our refuge and our strength, *mercifully* look down on Thy people who cry to Thee, and through the intercession of the glorious and immaculate Virgin Mary, Mother of God, of Saint Joseph her Spouse, of Thy blessed Apostles Peter and Paul, and of all the saints, in *mercy* and goodness hear our prayers."

After invoking St Michael, these Leonine Prayers end most fittingly with a triple invocation to Christ — not Christ as Judge or King, but Christ as Victim of love for our salvation. How telling that the very last petition addressed to God in Holy Mass should be to the Sacred Heart pierced for our sins! The Sacred Heart is our best assurance of securing divine mercy, which we so radically need. With filial assurance, then, we beg for mercy, a gift altogether unmerited and costly: "Most Sacred Heart of Jesus, have *mercy* on us! Most Sacred Heart of Jesus, have *mercy* on us! Most Sacred Heart of Jesus, have *mercy* on us!" By then, if we have received the Sacred Host in Holy Communion, Christ truly present in us is pouring upon our souls the mercies of the Father. What we ask for is to welcome His Real Presence in us with deep faith, and humbly to allow Him to bear abundant fruit in us, so that in our turn we may become "merciful like the Father."

8

Eucharistic Fragments

How Fragments Occur

Holy Mass is referred to in the New Testament as "breaking bread" or *fractio panis*: "And on the first day of the week, when we were assembled to break bread" (Acts 20:7; see also, e.g., Acts 2:42-46). This expression recalls the gesture of Jesus Himself when He instituted the Eucharistic sacrifice: "And taking bread, he gave thanks, and brake; and gave to them, saying: This is my body, which is given for you. Do this for a commemoration of me" (Luke 22:19). By destroying the unity of the loaf as a whole, the breaking of the bread expresses the death of the Victim, as would happen to a living creature similarly torn apart. Up to then, lambs and bulls would be ritually slaughtered, their lives offered up to God in atonement for the sin of the people. The two main physical components of those animals, their flesh and their blood, would be set apart; their flesh might be cut in smaller parts, and their blood might be sprinkled.

Fragmenting also allows sharing. The larger the number of pieces, the greater is the number of persons able to eat of it. Eating the sacrificial victim cleanses the contrite sinner and brings him back into communion with God, whom he has offended. But because man is a social being, his sin always harms the human community as well, so the shared eating of the victim also restores communion between those partaking in the sacrifice.

Thus, the breaking of the bread has a triple meaning: (1) it recalls the severing of the relationship between man and God through sin; (2) it expresses the death of the Victim whose vital unity is destroyed on behalf of the sinner; (3) it calls for reconciliation between men and God through atonement, and among men by allowing sharing of the sacrificial remedy.

Bread originates in a great number of separate grains of wheat gathered together and unified into a new whole through the process of milling and baking. The same applies to wine in relation to grapes. Every grain symbolically stands for a sinner, and every sinner who eats of the same bread offered in sacrifice is thus led back into harmony with God and in enhanced unity with his fellow men, by the virtue of the Eucharistic Sacrifice. So the oldest liturgical statement of the apostolic era (the *Didache* or "Doctrine of the twelve apostles," probably written in the years 65 to 80), states: "As this broken bread was scattered over the hills and then, when gathered, became one mass, so may Thy Church be gathered from the ends of the earth into Thy Kingdom" (9:4). Occasionally, the use of one very large host to be broken up and its sizable fragments distributed to the congregation in Holy Communion seeks to express this truth, although it increases the risk of losing some smaller fragments. Breaking obviously produces fragments, as the etymology illustrates. Indeed, the word "fragment" comes from the Latin noun *fragmentum*, itself derived from the Latin verb *frangere*, "to break."

Significantly, in both Eastern and Western liturgies, Eucharistic fragments soon became the focus of a specific liturgical rite called the Fermentum (the Latin word for "leaven"). The Fermentum is

> an ancient practise symbolising the unity of each local celebration of the Mass with that of the Bishop of Rome. For several centuries the Pope sent a particle of the consecrated bread from his celebration of Mass to each priest presiding at a local celebration, so that they would not be separated from communion with him. This particle (known as the *fermentum*) was then added to the chalice before the distribution of communion, to express the truth that the Eucharist is the sacrament of the unity of the Church. The term *fermentum* was possibly a reference to the Eucharist as the leaven of the Christian life, and the instrument by which Christians spread throughout the world were united in the one Body of Christ as a leaven in the world.[13]

Thus, from what we have seen, fragmenting the sacred Host is part and parcel of the Holy Sacrifice of the Mass, so that the existence of Eucharistic fragments at Mass is not an anomaly but a necessity. That point being settled, it remains to examine what those fragments are, since their identity will determine the appropriate way of dealing with them.

[13] Pontifical Committee for International Eucharistic Congresses, *The Eucharist: Communion with Christ and with One Another* (February 15, 2011), no. 114, https://www.vatican.va/roman _curia/pont_committees/eucharist-congr/documents/rc _committ_euchar_doc_20110215_50-testo-base_en.html.

What the Church Teaches

The Magisterium of the Church has constantly reaffirmed that from the moment the Consecration has taken place during Holy Mass, Christ is truly, really, and substantially present with His Body, Blood, Soul, and Divinity under the appearances (also called "species" or "accidents") of bread and wine, while the reality (or "substances") of bread and wine do not exist anymore under their mere appearances (having been replaced by the substances of the Body and Blood of Christ through transubstantiation). Specifically, the Church insists on the fact that Christ's presence does not depend on the size of the host or on the quantity of liquid in the Chalice. Whether the host is a very large one to be seen from afar, as at some Eucharistic congresses, or one of medium size as used by the celebrant, or a smaller one to be given to the communicants, there is simply no difference whatsoever as to the presence of Christ. Logically, this truth extends to fragments of the Host and to droplets of the Precious Blood.

Catechisms published by the Holy See are authoritative syntheses of the perennial Catholic Faith, designed not for expert theologians to debate upon, but for every baptized Catholic to hold firmly and to profess clearly. Consequently, any unnecessary or uncertain elements would be taken out. With this in mind, it is significant that the truth mentioned above has been found important enough to be affirmed in all such catechisms.

The latest catechism published was Pope Benedict XVI's *Compendium* in 2005. It teaches: "The breaking of the bread does not divide Christ. He is present whole and entire in each of the Eucharistic species and in each of their parts" (no. 284). In 1992, Pope John Paul II had stated in his *Catechism*

of the Catholic Church (CCC) that "Christ is present whole
and entire in each of the species and whole and entire in
each of their parts, in such a way that the breaking of the
bread does not divide Christ" (no. 1377). Before him, in
1908, Pope St. Pius X had affirmed in his own *Catechism
of Christian Doctrine:* "Yes, the same Jesus Christ is just as
much in a particle of a host as in a whole host" (q. 24). This
was no new doctrine; in 1566, the *Roman Catechism* of the
Council of Trent (and, to our knowledge, the first of its kind
ever published) also stated that "Christ, whole and entire,
is contained not only under either species, but also in each
particle of either species."

From very early on, the Church had professed that doctrine as a consequence logically drawn from the original
dogma of the Real Presence. Among many possible examples,
in the fourth century, St. Cyril of Jerusalem, in his *Catechetical Instructions*, explained how to receive the Sacred Host in
Holy Communion:

> Partake of it [the Holy Body]; giving heed lest you lose
> any portion thereof; for whatever you lose, is evidently
> a loss to you as it were from one of your own members.
> For tell me, if anyone gave you grains of gold, would
> you not hold them with all carefulness, being on your
> guard against losing any of them, and suffering loss?
> Will you not then much more carefully keep watch,
> that not a crumb fall from you of what is more pre-
> cious than gold and precious stones?

In the thirteenth, century, St. Thomas Aquinas wrote that
"Christ Himself, Perfect God and Perfect Man, Christ Himself
is there, under the appearance of a little bread and wine. His

faithful ones eat Him, but He is not mangled; nay, when [the veil which shroudeth Him in] this Sacrament is broken, in each broken piece thereof He remaineth whole."[14] The same Common Doctor of the Church insists most explicitly in his *Lauda Sion*: "Nor a single doubt retain, when they break the Host in twain, but that in each part remains what was in the whole before."[15] In his *Summa theologiae*, St. Thomas states that: "It is manifest that the entire Christ is under every part of the species of the bread."[16] To better appreciate the weight of St. Thomas's doctrinal authority, we recall Pope Benedict XVI's words in his General Audience of June 2, 2010:

> Today I wish to speak of the one whom the Church calls the *Doctor communis* — namely, St. Thomas Aquinas. In his Encyclical *Fides et Ratio* my venerable Predecessor, Pope John Paul II, recalled that "the Church has been justified in consistently proposing St. Thomas as a master of thought and a model of the right way to do theology" (no. 43). It is not surprising that, after St. Augustine, among the ecclesiastical writers mentioned in the *Catechism of the Catholic Church* St. Thomas is cited more than any other, at least 61 times."

Hence, St. Thomas Aquinas remains a most reliable Eucharistic guide, as is stressed by the Second Vatican Council:

---

[14] Matins of Corpus Christi, fifth reading: "Manducatur itaque a fidelibus, sed minime laceratur; quinnimo, diviso sacramento, sub qualibet divisionis particula integer perseverat."

[15] "Fracto demum sacramento, ne vacilles, sed memento, tantum esse sub fragmento, quantum toto tegitur."

[16] *Summa theologiae* III, q. 76, art. 3.

"Next, in order that they may shed light on the mysteries of salvation as completely as possible, the students [i.e., for the priesthood] should learn to penetrate them more deeply with the help of speculation, with St. Thomas as their master, and to perceive their interconnections."[17] The council further praised: "The example of the doctors of the Church and especially of St. Thomas Aquinas."[18]

The Testimony of Holy Scripture

In the New Testament, Our Lord states unequivocally that He gives His true self in the Holy Eucharist:

> Amen, amen I say unto you: Except you eat the flesh of the Son of man, and drink his blood, you shall not have life in you. He that eateth my flesh, and drinketh my blood, hath everlasting life: and I will raise him up in the last day. For my flesh is meat indeed: and my blood is drink indeed. He that eateth my flesh, and drinketh my blood, abideth in me, and I in him. (John 6:54-57 [53-56])

One may object, pointing out the fact that no literal indication is here provided as to Christ's abiding presence in consecrated fragments. But prior to this Eucharistic revelation, on two occasions, Our Lord miraculously multiplied a few loaves to feed thousands of people. There is no doubt that Jesus intended those miracles to prepare the crowds to accept the

---

[17] Second Vatican Council, Decree on Priestly Training *Optatam totius* (October 28, 1965), no. 16.

[18] Second Vatican Council, Declaration on Christian Education *Gravissimum educationis* (October 28, 1965), no. 10.

difficult doctrine of the Eucharist. In this perspective, let us see whether the evangelists mention any fragments of bread.

St. Matthew: "And taking the seven loaves and the fishes, and giving thanks, he brake, and gave to his disciples, and the disciples to the people. And they did all eat, and had their fill. And they took up seven baskets full, of what remained of the *fragments*" (15:36–37). St. Mark: "They took up that which was left of the *fragments*, seven baskets" (8:8). St. Luke: "And they did all eat, and were filled. And there were taken up of *fragments* that remained to them, twelve baskets" (9:17) (all emphases ours).

As we can see, the three first evangelists are very explicit about the care taken by the Apostles to gather up the fragments of bread. But we know that their narratives are generally similar, whereas St. John's Gospel often omits elements mentioned by his fellow evangelists, focusing on other aspects to provide a complementary outlook. Not in this case though: "When they were filled, he said to his disciples: Gather up the *fragments* that remain, lest they be lost. They gathered up therefore, and filled twelve baskets with the *fragments* of the five barley loaves, which remained over and above to them that had eaten" (6:12–13).

Thus, not only does St. John's Gospel mention the gathering of the fragments of miraculous bread, just as the three other Gospels do, but it further adds that such gathering up was no zealous initiative by the Apostles, but rather a command from the Lord Himself to them: "Gather up the *fragments* that remain, lest they be lost." Furthermore, later on Our Lord Himself refers to His two miracles of the multiplication of loaves. Strikingly, on both occasions He points to the gathering of the fragments: "When I broke the five loaves among five thousand, how many baskets full of fragments took you up? They say to him, 'Twelve.' 'When also the seven loaves among four thousand, how many baskets of fragments took you up?' And they say to him, 'Seven' " (Mark 8:19-20). From this we can conclude that the gathering of fragments of multiplied bread (1) is a constant feature in those miracles; (2) is personally commanded by the Lord to His Apostles; and (3) is subsequently pointed to by the Lord. This shows that the gathering up of fragments was important to Jesus and was understood as such by all the four evangelists. For what reason? Could the Lord's insistence merely express a domestic concern about avoiding waste of food? Certainly Our Lord would not have wanted the crowds to show contempt or carelessness for the food provided. But given the enormous quantity of bread miraculously and generously offered, domestic economy cannot be the main motive here. Rather, Christ wishes to inculcate respect—even accountability—for each fragment of the miraculous bread produced, irrespective of quantity or size. Bearing in mind that every episode in the life of Jesus was a preparation for His Hour, that of His Passion and death, it is certain that when multiplying bread, He would have known in advance the gestures of His forthcoming First Mass when, the night He was betrayed, He would similarly take bread, bless, *break*, and give to His disciples to eat.

After the Ascension, when the Apostles and the first Christian communities began "to break the bread" (i.e., to offer Mass) after the example of the Lord, they knew and believed in the reality of His presence under the Eucharistic appearances. Gradually they drew the liturgical consequences of this truth, giving instructions to prevent any consecrated fragment (and any droplet of Precious Blood) from being lost. They would remember the Lord's insistence on this point after the two miracles of the multiplication of the loaves and would then realize how the supreme gift of the Eucharistic presence brought with it an accountability of love for each particle.

On two other occasions in the Holy Bible, we read about the same special consideration expressed by God for mere crumbs. The first is in Exodus 16:13-21, when manna, miraculous bread again, is sent to the Hebrews starving in the desert. Moses commands them on behalf of God: "Let no man leave thereof till the morning." By this warning, God intends to teach His people to trust in His providence and obey His will as spelled out by Moses, His appointed intermediary. This essential trust in God, who miraculously feeds His children, is manifested through consuming every fragment of bread. God will provide anew on the morrow, but for the present time, the allotted quantity must be consumed completely. It is well known that the manna was intended by God to prefigure the true celestial bread, the one providing everlasting life to souls. Thus, this episode in the book of Exodus prepares our correct understanding of the Eucharistic fragments. The second episode, in the New Testament, we will see later on.

Some Rubrics of the Mass

"Gather up the fragments!" (John 6:12). With diligence, Holy Mother Church repeats those very words of her Divine Spouse, when at Mass, after Consecration and Communion, she instructs the priest acting *in persona Christi* as follows:

The celebrant "takes the paten, inspects the corporal, *gathers up the fragments* with the paten if any are to be found; with the thumb and index of his right hand, he also cleanses the paten above the chalice as well as his fingers, lest any fragment may stay on them.[19]

The Ordinary Form Roman Missal similarly states:

Upon returning to the altar, the Priest *collects the fragments*, should any remain, and he stands at the altar or at the credence table and purifies the paten or ciborium over the chalice, and after this purifies the chalice, saying quietly the formula *Quod ore sumpsimus Domine* (What has passed our lips), and dries the chalice with a purificator.[20]

Following the example of Our Lord in reference to the fragments of bread miraculously multiplied, the Church stresses conscientiousness but does not encourage scrupulosity. Indeed, after the multiplication of the loaves for five thousand men, Jesus did not command the Apostles to spend hours combing the grass for every last particle of bread. Simply, whatever could be identified as bread and conveniently seized had to be gathered up.

Much smaller are the scale and dimensions of an altar, inside a church, for an average congregation of communicants. Preventing the loss of fragments of consecrated hosts is thus much easier. To refer further to the 1962 Roman Missal, the

---

[19] "Accipit [celebrans] patenam, inspicit corporale, colligit fragmenta cum patena, si quae sint in eo: patenam quoque cum pollice et indice dexterae manus super calicem extergit et ipsos digitos, ne quid fragmentorum in eis remaneat." Rubrics of the Extraordinary Form Roman Missal.

[20] *General Instruction of the Roman Missal* (GIRM), chap. 4, no. 163.

successive gestures prescribed by the liturgy are enough to assure the celebrant that he has acted appropriately. Thus, from the moment of Consecration, the celebrant is required "not to disjoin his thumbs and index fingers up to the ablution of the fingers after the Communion, except when he must touch or handle the consecrated Host," lest some fragments adhering to the tips of his fingers might inadvertently transfer to the objects he would touch, such as to the pages of the missal, the stems of the chalice and ciborium, or the vestments and altar cloth outside the corporal.

Significantly, chalices and ciboria designed for the older form of the Mass purposely keep the foot and cup at some distance from the knob (halfway between them on the stem), so that with one hand the celebrant may comfortably hold it with his middle, third, and little fingers on the one side and his joined index and thumb on the other. For the same reason, over the chalice the celebrant must "wipe his fingers, which he should always do if a few fragments adhere to his fingers," so that they may fall into the chalice and be consumed rather than be lost. After the celebrant has given Holy Communion, "if there have been any hosts upon the corporal, he scrapes it with the paten, and if there are fragments upon it, places them in the chalice.... Afterward he places in the chalice any fragments which he happens to find upon the paten, which was placed under the mouths of the communicants."

This liturgical care for fragments of consecrated host is also manifest in the rite of cleaning the sacred linens. Thus, when ordaining subdeacons, the bishop instructs them "to clean the altar cloths and the corporals," specifying that "the cloths which cover the altar must be washed in a vase and the corporals in another. Where the corporals have been washed, no other linen must be washed. The used water must be poured in the sacrarium." (The sacrarium is a hole in a stone recess near the altar, channeling blessed liquids directly to the soil, separately from any drain network.) The reason for the even greater care and reverence required for washing corporals is the likeliness of very small Eucharistic fragments remaining in their folds even after they were last scraped by the celebrant at Mass. They would dissolve once immersed in the water. In the absence of a sacrarium, the water used may be reverently spread by the cleric across un-trodden grass or soil.

Because God has designed the Holy Eucharist solely for us human beings, He expects us to take reasonable care of Him in each Eucharistic fragment in proportion with the size of human fingers and within the range of human senses. Provided one has carefully followed the rubrics, giving way to scruples would not fulfill the Church's intention.

Conclusion

To conclude this article on the Eucharistic fragments, let us go back to the New Testament. In St. Matthew's and St. Mark's Gospels, a non-Jewish woman receives divine assistance when begging humbly even for mere "crumbs" of God's grace:

> And behold a woman of Canaan who came out of those coasts, crying out, said to him: Have mercy on me, O Lord, thou son of David: my daughter is griev-ously troubled by the devil. Who answered her not a word. And his disciples came and besought him, saying: Send her away, for she crieth after us: And

he answering, said: I was not sent but to the sheep that are lost of the house of Israel. But she came and adored him, saying: Lord, help me. Who answering, said: It is not good to take the bread of the children, and to cast it to the dogs. But she said: Yea, Lord; for the whelps also eat of *the crumbs that fall* from the table of their masters. Then Jesus answering, said to her: O woman, great is thy faith: be it done to thee as thou wilt: and her daughter was cured from that hour. (Matt. 15:22–28)

No reference to the Eucharist is made here, but both St. Matthew and St. Mark place this episode shortly before the multiplication of loaves quoted above. Bearing in mind Jesus' attention to miraculous crumbs, it sounds as if the woman's humble begging even for fallen crumbs had unlocked the Savior's assistance after His initial refusal. In the Canaanite's petition, the "children" are those who by right enjoy access to the bread destined for them. They are not careful enough though to prevent crumbs from falling from the table onto the ground. The house pets will be happy enough to eat them. In His rebuke to the woman, Jesus uses the word "bread" metaphorically for "grace," i.e., divine power applied to the needs of men. The woman values God's assistance to the extent that mere residues of His power are priceless to her. Because in humility and faith she cared for the crumbs, instead of being cast away like a dog, she merited to be rewarded as a lawful child.

9

On Concomitance: "Is Christ Divided?"

In this essay, we reflect on the connection between Christ's Body and Blood in the Holy Eucharist. On the one hand, we have the hosts. On the other hand, we have the Chalice. Our eyes see them as separate. We thus ask ourselves: "Is Christ divided?"

Unity in the Church

St. Paul bears witness to the unity of Christ according to His Mystical Body, the Church. He stresses that Christians are all one in Christ.

Now I beseech you, brethren, by the name of our Lord Jesus Christ, that you all speak the same thing, and that there be no schisms among you; but that you be perfect in the same mind, and in the same judgment. For it hath been signified unto me, my brethren, of you, by them that are of the house of Chloe, that there are contentions among you. Now this I say, that every one of you saith: I indeed am of Paul; and I am of Apollo; and I am of Cephas; and I of Christ. Is Christ divided? Was Paul then crucified for you? or were you baptized in the name of Paul? I give God thanks, that I baptized none of you but Crispus and Caius; Lest any should say that you were baptized in my name. (1 Cor. 1:10-15)

What applies to Christ in His Mystical Body, the Church, should apply as well to His Eucharistic Body. To a greater extent even must Christ be one in the Holy Eucharist, because such unity is the principle for the unity of His members with Him and among themselves. Let us see how.

What do healthy persons, families, and countries have in common? Unity. Free from internal fracture or strife, they develop and act as harmonious wholes. Unity denotes life. On the contrary, disunity indicates death and physical, moral, or social decay.

God, who is life itself, is supremely one: an undivided Communion of Persons. God's creation reflected His unity. Adam and Eve were created in a state of communion with God. Through grace, God granted our first parents a created sharing in His own life and unity. When they sinned, losing the life of grace, they lost unity. Adam's divorce from God damaged all his subordinate relationships: with Eve (as expressed through accusation and concupiscence), with nature (arduousness of labor and pangs of childbirth), and within his soul (the will opposing the intellect). A definitively striking expression of such lost unity was Adam's death. The basic components of his being went their separate ways; that is, his soul left his body, through which his blood ceased to flow.

The New Adam, Our Blessed Lord Jesus Christ, restored the broken unity of the human race, enhancing it even. In His Person, human nature was substantially united with God.

Later on, to atone for our sins, Jesus suffered and died. His Soul, His Body, and His Blood were separated from each other. But on Easter morning, those three basic components of His humanity were brought together again forever through His Resurrection, principle and pledge of our resurrection. By His own institution, Our Blessed Lord's saving death is made present again in the Holy Sacrifice of the Mass. The separate Consecrations of His Body first, and then of His Blood, express the radical separation of the solid and liquid components of His humanity, as occurred once on Golgotha. But Our Lord is present in the Most Holy Eucharist as risen, not as dead. Therefore, the unity of His Body, Blood, Soul, and Divinity must exist in this sacrament, even under the separate appearances of bread and wine. In this article, we will consider how the Church has learned to discern in the Holy Eucharist this necessary unity of her Risen Spouse, Jesus, Restorer of life and Life Himself.

Four Components

When did Our Lady receive Holy Communion for the very first time? Moving as this thought is, it refers to a historical fact. One day, the Mother of God was given her very Son again, under the appearances of bread and wine. At the latest, this would have occurred when she was settled in Ephesus with St. John, whose offering of the Eucharistic Sacrifice she would have attended. Could this have occurred even before the Resurrection—on Holy Saturday? What a consolation our Most Sorrowful Mother would have drawn from it! St. Thomas Aquinas mentions this hypothesis, but he points out that "had this sacrament been celebrated during those three days when He was dead, the soul of Christ would not have been there,"[21] for it was in Limbo, visiting the just (what is known as the Harrowing of Hell). Furthermore, the Body and Blood of Jesus were temporally disjoined—the former in the Tomb and the latter scattered across Jerusalem—so that the Host would have been Jesus' Body (and Godhead) without His Blood, and the Chalice would have contained Jesus' Blood (and Godhead) without His Body. In this instance, Communion under both kinds would have been necessary for Our Lady to receive the Body of Jesus together with His Blood; but His Soul would have been missing.

Consequently, this mode of receiving her Son within her would have been less perfect than on the day of the Annunciation when, from the Holy Ghost, the Blessed Virgin Mary had conceived Jesus as a living whole, with His Body, Blood, Soul, and Divinity intimately united. So she had carried Him in her virginal womb during nine months. The New Adam, God the Son made man, had then developed in Mary with all that pertains to human nature—i.e., with a created body irrigated by blood, both kept together by a spiritual soul. Alas, His sorrowful Passion endured for our sins had violently detached His Soul from His lacerated Body and drained from His Body nearly all His Blood.

As to Christ's Godhead, we know that it had remained united, on the one hand, to His Body while lying in the sepulcher, thus preserving it from decay; and, on the other hand, to His Soul, when He descended into Limbo. This truth is very important to us, as it demonstrates that God has never repudiated our human nature after He had espoused it at the Incarnation.

---

[21] See *Summa theologiae* III, q. 76, art. 1.

St. Thomas Aquinas explains it as follows:

What belongs to the body of Christ after death is predi-
cated of the Son of God—namely, being buried: as is
evident from the Creed, in which it is said that the Son
of God "was conceived and born of a Virgin, suffered,
died, and was buried." Therefore Christ's Godhead
was not separated from the flesh when He died....
The Word of God was not separated from the body at
Christ's death, much less was He separated from the
soul. Accordingly, since what regards the body severed
from the soul is affirmed of the Son of God—namely,
that "it was buried"—so is it said of Him in the Creed
that "He descended into hell," because His soul when
separated from the body did go down into hell.[22]

Hence, during those three days, even though still united
to the Divine Person of God the Son, Christ's Body, Blood,
and Soul were separated from each other. But His lost unity
was forever restored from the moment of His Resurrection,
as St. Thomas Aquinas shows:

Now it is clear that flesh, bones, blood, and other
such things, are of the very nature of the human body.
Consequently, all these things were in Christ's body
when He rose again; and this also integrally, without
any diminution; otherwise it would not have been a
complete resurrection, if whatever was lost by death
had not been restored.... All the blood which flowed
from Christ's body, belonging as it does to the integrity

[22] *Summa theologiae* III, q. 50, arts. 2, 3.

of human nature, rose again with His body: and the same reason holds good for all the particles which belong to the truth and integrity of human nature.[23]

Hence, the four components in Christ—Body, Blood, Soul, and Divinity—were united again and ever after would remain so. The three created human elements (Body, Blood, and Soul) will never again be separated from each other or from the Divinity.

It is fitting, then, that no Mass should have been offered until after the Resurrection. When St. John or St. Peter offered Holy Mass for the first time, Our Blessed Lady received Holy Communion from one of them, with perfect devotion and with the deepest faith ever in the reality of the substantial presence of her Son, with His Body, Blood, Soul, and Divinity, under the appearances of bread and wine. At Holy Mass indeed, Jesus gives Himself to us as Victim offered to the Father for our sins, but also as risen for our salvation. Therefore, under the externals of bread and wine, it is undoubtedly Christ, whole and alive, whom we receive, with His true human Body, His Precious Blood, and His immaculate Soul, united with each other and with the Divinity.

Under Both Kinds

Communion under both kinds was certainly common among early Christians. They believed in the sacramental change of the bread into the Body of Christ and of the wine into His Blood. They knew that the separate Consecrations of the host and of the Chalice expressed the death of the Lord on the Cross, when His Body and His Blood were separated.

---

[23] *Summa theologiae* III, q. 54, art. 3.

They accepted the very words of Jesus, transmitted by the Apostles, affirming that after the double Consecration, He was present truly, not symbolically. Led by love, the Church gradually unfolded more layers of the Eucharistic mystery. Guided by the Holy Ghost, she understood that even though the externals of bread and wine remain, in the Consecration of the host the change is from the substance of the bread into that of the Body of Christ; whereas in the Consecration of the Chalice, the change is from the substance of the wine into that of the Precious Blood of Christ.

But the Church also knew that the Holy Eucharist is Christ risen, not Christ dead. Christ meant to give Himself to His people alive—i.e., with His Body, Blood, Soul, and Divinity intrinsically united. Admittedly, right after receiving both kinds of Communion—the Host and the Precious Blood—Christ's Body and Blood were brought together within the person of the communicant swallowing the Sacred Species. But that was an extrinsic and somehow accidental unity. As Christ is present in the Eucharist as risen, the unity of His Body, Blood, Soul, and Divinity pre-exists our receiving Him. His unity has to be the very gift received by us in Holy Communion, rather than a consequence of our communicating. Otherwise, if, for some reason, no one were to communicate, then Christ would still be disjoined in the Eucharist.

So, how did this vital unity occur, as the bread was transubstantiated into the Body only, and the wine into the Blood only? What of the Blood, Soul, and Divinity in relation to the Host? What of the Body, Soul, and Divinity in relation to the Chalice? The Body would not save communicants unless it were alive, and it could not be alive unless it contained Blood, so that Christ's Precious Blood must have accompanied His

Body even in the Host. But the same Body and Blood would still not be alive, unless they were animated by a Soul, causing the Blood to circulate throughout the Body, so that Christ's Soul as well had to accompany His Body and Blood in the Host.

If, under the solid externals of bread, the substance of Christ's solid Body was accompanied by His liquid Blood and spiritual Soul, then reciprocally, under the liquid externals of wine in the Chalice, the substance of Christ's liquid Blood had to be accompanied by His solid Body and spiritual Soul. Thus, the solid, liquid and spiritual components of Christ's humanity (respectively, His Body, Blood, and Soul) were understood to be brought together in the Host, and equally in the Chalice, through the Eucharistic change. But Christ is God the Son made Man. His Divinity, then, had to accompany His human nature as well.

Concomitance

Let us recapitulate. "Accompaniment" was the name given by Holy Mother Church to articulate transubstantiation and unity. As regards the Host, transubstantiation is strictly from the bread to the Body, but, for the sake of the vital unity of the risen Christ, the Body is accompanied by the Blood, Soul, and Divinity. Likewise, as regards the Chalice, transubstantiation is strictly from the wine to the Blood, but, for the sake of the vital unity of the risen Christ, the Blood is accompanied by the Body, Soul, and Divinity. In Latin, "accompaniment" translates as *concomitantia*, whence comes our modern word "concomitance." The Council of Trent wrote as follows:

> This faith has ever been in the Church of God, that, immediately after the consecration, the veritable Body

of our Lord, and His veritable Blood, together with His soul and divinity, are under the species [i.e., externals or appearances] of bread and wine; but the Body indeed under the species of bread, and the Blood under the species of wine, by the force of the words [of Consecration]; but the body itself under the species of wine, and the blood under the species of bread, and the soul under both, by the force of that natural connexion and concomitance whereby the parts of Christ our Lord, who hath now risen from the dead, to die no more, are united together; and the divinity, furthermore, on account of the admirable hypostatical union thereof with His body and soul. Wherefore it is most true, that as much is contained under either species as under both; for Christ whole and entire is under the species of bread, and under any part whatsoever of that species; likewise the whole (Christ) is under the species of wine, and under the parts thereof.[24]

To our early Christian forefathers, whenever circumstances allowed, Communion under both kinds would manifest more eloquently the sacrificial nature of the Eucharistic Food. Speaking generally, when, through their physical senses, communicants see, smell, taste, and eventually swallow Christ under the externals of bread and also of wine, the separation between His Body and His Soul is more vividly expressed, His subsequent death as Victim is more deeply recalled and contrition for the sins that caused His Passion is more acutely aroused. However, clergy and laity alike know that the weakness of our nature makes us very prone to distraction even at the time of Communion, so

[24] Council of Trent, Session 13, chap. 3.

that receiving also from the Chalice—as celebrants do at every Mass—does not guarantee a more fruitful Communion than receiving the Host only. Rather, the fruit of sacramental Communion depends on how ardent the faith of the communicant is and on how lovingly he has prepared his soul through the sacramental absolution of any mortal sin and through fasting. What of the first Christians, then, in that regard?

The earliest description of Holy Mass after the Last Supper is given to us by St. Paul in his First Letter to the Corinthians. The Apostle warns them in the strongest terms: "Whosoever shall eat this bread, *or* drink the chalice of the Lord unworthily, shall be guilty of the body *and* of the blood of the Lord.... He that eateth and drinketh unworthily, eateth and drinketh judgment to himself, not discerning the body of the Lord" (1 Cor. 11:27, 29). An unworthy Communion from the Host *or* from the Chalice (separately) makes the person guilty of the Body *and* of the Blood of the Lord (jointly): "and" refers back to "or." In other words, even though unworthy Communion to the Host is considered *separately* from unworthy Communion from the Chalice, yet the guilt pertains to the Body *and* to the Blood *together*.

Admittedly, St. Paul was not expounding here the doctrine of concomitance, as it was elaborated only later on. Yet, as Rev. Joseph McRory (later cardinal archbishop of Armagh) commented: "Since, then, both body and blood are here shown to be contained under either species, this verse has always been urged against the Utraquists as evidence that Communion under both kinds is not necessary."[25]

---

[25] Joseph McRory, *The Epistles of St Paul to the Corinthians* (Dublin, 1915), 177.

Loving Care

Communion by means of the Host alone was known from early Christian times. The Fathers of the Church and archaeological monuments provide ample evidence of Holy Communion being brought to the sick and to the persecuted without its liquid form; and of the Blessed Sacrament being reserved at home under the sole appearance of bread. This would not have been possible unless early Christians believed that Communion from the Host alone secured the same graces as Communion under both kinds. As awareness grew of the Real Presence of the Beloved Savior not only in the Host and Chalice as a whole, but even in any identifiable fragment of Host or in any droplet of Precious Blood, loving care increased and liturgical precautions developed for a safe and reverent handling of so great a treasure. This loving concern about the hazards that might affect the Host and Chalice, and how to act in such cases, was best expressed from the sixteenth century onward in the Roman Missal:

> If through negligence any of the Blood of Christ is spilt, and it falls on the ground or on the table of the altar, it should be licked up with the tongue, and the place itself scraped as much as necessary, and the scraping burnt, and the ashes thrown into the sacrarium. If it falls on the altar stone, the priest should mop up the spot, and the spot should be well washed, and the ablution thrown into the sacrarium. If on the altar linen, and it soaks through to the second or third cloth, the cloths should be thrice washed where the drop fell, with the chalice underneath, and the water of the washing thrown into the sacrarium. If on the

corporal alone, or on the priest's vestments, they must be washed in the same way, and the ablution thrown into the sacrarium. If on the cloth or carpet underfoot, that too must be well washed in the manner just described.... If it should happen that all the Blood is spilt after the consecration: any that remains, however little, should be swallowed, and the priest should deal with the rest in accordance with the above directions.... If the consecrated host, or any particle of it, falls on the ground, it should be reverently taken up, and the place where it fell washed and slightly scraped, the dot or scraping being put into the sacrarium. If it falls outside the corporal on the altar cloth, or otherwise on any linen, such cloth or linen should be carefully washed, and the water used for washing thrown into the sacrarium.[26]

The Missal of St. John XXIII, currently in force as the Extraordinary Form of the Roman Rite, has retained most of those precautions, and several are still explicitly mentioned in reference to Holy Mass in the Ordinary Form. For instance: "The Communion-plate for the Communion of the faithful should be retained, so as to avoid the danger of the sacred host or some fragment of it falling";[27] and further: "the pouring of the Blood of Christ after the consecration from one vessel to another is completely to be avoided, lest

[26] *De Defectibus*, chap. 4, X, 12–13, 15.
[27] Congregation for Divine Worship and the Discipline of the Sacrament, instruction *Redemptionis Sacramentum* (April 23, 2004), no. 93, referring to *GIRM* 180.

anything should happen that would be to the detriment of so great a mystery."[28]

The truth is that a liquid is much more likely to spread than a solid is likely to crumble. Those same laws of physics experienced at home will also apply in church. The physical structure of a liquid makes its level always unstable inside a container and, as soon as it is spilt, it will quickly spread. Admittedly, mercury or thick oil tends to coalesce. Wine on the other hand will permeate the cloth or carpet and will run into any crack of the wood or stone. Since the externals of wine denote the Precious Blood irrespective of quantity (whether a full chalice or a mere droplet), the risk for it to be lost on lips or chin and to fall upon clothes or on the floor is actually much higher than for Hosts or fragments of Hosts. Those very practical considerations led to gradually restricting Communion from the Chalice.

In the sixteenth century, the Council of Trent did not innovate when systematizing the liturgical precautions mentioned above; neither were they imposed by Rome as if alien to local customs. In diverse ways, they were implemented centuries earlier in many dioceses and local churches across Christendom. In England, for instance, the Synod of Lambeth stipulated in 1281 that Communion from the Chalice should not be offered to the congregation. This was by no means intended to deprive the people of Eucharistic graces, since those are secured even when communicating by the Host only, but rather to prevent accidents, which are more likely to occur when a liquid is presented to various communicants to drink from the same vessel.

[28] *Redemptionis Sacramentum* 106.

Teach This Truth

Seven hundred years later, the *Catechism of the Catholic Church*, published by Pope St. John Paul II, stated the same principle: "Since Christ is sacramentally present under each of the species, communion under the species of bread alone makes it possible to receive all the fruit of Eucharistic grace. For pastoral reasons this manner of receiving communion has been legitimately established as the most common form in the Latin rite" (1390). A few years ago in England, during the so-called swine flu outbreak, some bishops forbade Communion from the Chalice at Mass for fear of contamination. They rightly deemed Communion under the species of bread sufficient to convey every Eucharistic grace required.

The Ordinary Form Roman Missal similarly stresses the link between this doctrine and its liturgical consequences:

> Sacred pastors should take care to ensure that the faithful who participate in the rite or are present at it are as fully aware as possible of the Catholic teaching on the form of Holy Communion as set forth by the Ecumenical Council of Trent. Above all, they should instruct the Christian faithful that the Catholic faith teaches that Christ, whole and entire, and the true Sacrament, is received even under only one species, and consequently that as far as the effects are concerned, those who receive under only one species are not deprived of any of the grace that is necessary for salvation.... Any of the faithful who wish to receive Holy Communion under the species of bread alone should be granted their wish.[29]

[29] GIRM 282, 284.

On September 1, 1425, Pope Martin V confirmed the following decree issued by the Council of Constance in 1415:

> Although this sacrament was received by the faithful in the early Church under both species, nevertheless this custom has been reasonably introduced to avoid certain dangers and scandals, namely, that it be received by those who consecrate it under both species, and by the laity only under the species of bread, since it must be believed most firmly and not at all doubted that the whole body of Christ and the blood are truly contained under the species of bread as well as under the species of wine.

Stressing that this custom had been "introduced for good reasons by the Church and holy fathers, and has been observed for a very long time," the Council pronounced in favor of its continuance, which shows that Communion under both kinds had fallen into disuse at least several centuries earlier.

Before I conclude, let us remember that the very words of Christ in the Holy Gospels do not purport that Communion under both kinds should be necessary:

> Neither is it rightly gathered, from that discourse which is in the sixth of John—however according to the various interpretations of holy Fathers and Doctors it be understood—that the communion of both species was enjoined by the Lord: for He who said: Except you eat the flesh of the Son of Man and drink his blood, you shall not have life in you (v. 54), also said: He that eateth this bread shall live for ever (v.

59); and He who said: He that eateth my flesh and drinketh my blood hath everlasting life (v. 55), also said: The bread that I will give is my flesh for the life of the world (v. 52); and, in fine—He who said: He that eateth my flesh and drinketh my blood, abideth in me and I in him (v. 57), said, nevertheless: He that eateth this bread shall live for ever (v. 59).[30]

Two chapters later, the same Council confirms:

Although, as hath been already said, our Redeemer, in that last supper, instituted, and delivered to the apostles, this sacrament in two species, yet is to be acknowledged, that Christ whole and entire and a true sacrament are received under either species alone; and that therefore, as regards the fruit thereof, they, who receive one species alone, are not defrauded of any grace necessary to salvation.

Conclusion

Those theological considerations and their liturgical consequences truly deepen our faith when understood according to the loving heart of the Church, the mystical Bride of Christ, caring for her Beloved Spouse truly present in the Holy Eucharist. The Holy Eucharist is the Mystery of Faith. In harmony with reason, a deep faith is required of all to believe that, under what our senses identify as bread and wine, the true Body, Blood, Soul, and Divinity of Christ are present. Blessed Pope Paul VI describes this presence as "ontological"

---

[30] Council of Trent, Session 21, chap. I.

and this difficult act of faith as "especially meritorious."[31] Once it is made, all the work is done.

Faith in the doctrine of concomitance is but a logical consequence of a more fundamental truth already embraced, that of the Real Presence. Similarly, once we believe the stupendous statement that God has become man, we should have very little difficulty in accepting the circumstances of His Birth of a Virgin, in a stable, and of His being laid in a manger. We have seen the logical reasons for the enlightening doctrine of concomitance. May it arouse our gratitude toward our Savior, who once espoused our human nature and never repudiated it, even in the tomb. May this truth strengthen our faith in the unity of His Body, Blood, Soul, and Divinity, restored at His Resurrection as a pledge of our own rising. May we further acknowledge the same unity made present at every Mass from the moment of Consecration, under either species and in any fragment or drop. And may the Most Holy Virgin Mary, who gave us Jesus, be our guide in Eucharistic love for her Son, our Lord.

[31] Pope St. Paul VI, encyclical letter *Mysterium Fidei* (September 3, 1965), 46 and 20.

10

The Formulas of Consecration

Introduction

When a priest utters the sacred words of Consecration during Holy Mass, a greater wonder occurs than the creation of the whole universe. Through His human intermediary, the Creator and Redeemer of the world makes Himself truly present in the hands of His priest, under the externals of bread and wine. Christ operates this great change from bread and wine to His Body and Blood. He does it to make us participants in His unique Sacrifice on the Cross, reenacted at every Holy Mass. If we attend with faith and devotion, the saving merits that Our Lord acquired on our behalf through His sorrowful Passion and death are applied to the wounds of our souls, our sins. Who would not agree that those words of Consecration are of immense importance? Is it not legitimate to ensure that they are uttered as faithfully and purposely as possible?

To that end, this article will examine the words, gestures, and punctuation of the formulas of Eucharistic Consecration, in either form of the Roman Missal. This will entail comparisons between various versions of the traditional Roman missal and the new one. I offer these solely as an attempt to find out what liturgical signs better help souls adhere in faith to the sacrificial nature of Holy Mass and to the reality of Christ's presence occurring at the Consecration. I hope that my attention to detail will not seem unduly punctilious. Rather, I invite the reader to join me in a spiritual outlook upon such salutary minutiae. We shall be in good company, including, among many others, St. Teresa of Avila, who wrote in her autobiography: "I knew well enough that in matters of faith I would not break the least ceremony of the Church, that I would expose myself to die a thousand times rather than that any one should see me go against it" (chap. 33).

Not Literally

Very few priests, if any, use the very words spoken by the Lord Jesus when He first offered Mass on Maundy Thursday. On that solemn occasion in the Upper Room, in Jerusalem, Christ said in Aramaic the words soon after quoted by St. Paul in Greek, later translated into Latin and finally repeated in all the languages on Earth:

> For I have received of the Lord that which also I delivered unto you, that the Lord Jesus, the same night in which he was betrayed, took bread. And giving thanks, broke, and said: *Take ye, and eat: this is my body, which shall be delivered for you: this do for the commemoration of me.* In like manner also the chalice, after he had supped, saying: *This chalice is the new testament in my blood: this do ye, as often as you shall drink, for the commemoration of me.* For as often as you shall eat this bread, and drink the chalice, you shall shew the death of the Lord, until he come. (1 Cor. 11:23-26)

Early on, perhaps even from the time of the Apostles, priests would have started repeating those sacred words in their native tongue rather than in the original Aramaic. This first alteration undergone by the words of Consecration was obviously allowed by Church authorities, assured that it would not affect the efficacy of the formulas. Whether Greek or any other language was used, the bread and wine would still be changed into the Body and Blood of the Lord. This simple fact shows that fidelity to the intention and to the mandate of the Lord was not understood by the early Church as a literal repetition, forbidding the smallest modification.

Based on that sound principle, theologians stated that minor alterations in uttering the formulas—due, for instance, to an accidental distraction of the celebrant or to his unclear pronunciation—would not affect the validity of the Consecration. While this relieves scrupulous Catholics, it is not meant to condone negligence in so crucial a rite. On the contrary, the Roman Missal instructs the celebrant to pronounce the sacred words "distinctly, reverently, and secretly"—adding the adverb "continuously" for the longer formula of Consecration of the Precious Blood. Regardless of minor alterations to the formulas of Consecration, whether accidental or magisterial, the fact is that those two sequences of words are endowed by God with an efficacy beyond human capacity. For they change bread and wine into God's Body and Blood. What can be greater than that?

Many other words are spoken by the priest celebrant from the beginning of Mass until its end, sometimes alone, sometimes with the congregation. One may recall the Kyrie, the Gloria, the Creed, the various Offertory prayers, and those of the Canon and Communion. They are inspired words, grouped in sublime invocations to the Holy Trinity, stating the Faith of the Church with precision, strength, and beauty. But they do not operate the transubstantiation. Only the double formula of Consecration has that power. This difference sets the two Consecration formulas apart from all the other prayers of the Mass (and indeed, from any word ever uttered by men on earth, except Our Lady's Fiat at the Annunciation). The two formulas of Consecration shine as twin jewels enshrined in the texts of the Mass. All other prayers lead to those two and stem from them. Reciprocally, the double formula fulfills the other prayers, bringing about the sacrificial and saving presence of Christ upon the altar, whence it is available for Holy Communion.

On the page of the altar missal used by her priests, the Church enhances visually the distinctive status of the Consecration formulas. The words of Consecration stand out, sometimes in block capitals, centered, and of a larger size than the words before and after. This striking layout reminds the celebrant at a glance that he is nearing the most important part of the Mass. When he starts uttering the sacred formulas, the divine power embedded in his soul (through the sacerdotal character received at his priestly ordination) will be activated. And bread and wine will be turned into the Body and Blood of God.

But this momentous change is not visible. In the celebrant's hands, the Host retains exactly the same round shape, white color, and frail texture as a few seconds earlier, before the sacred words were uttered. The celebrant does not see Christ in his hands; neither do we. This most radical change of all escapes our physical senses. But it does not escape our faith. Our God-revealed Faith, grounded on sound philosophy and illustrated by the virtues of countless saints, does show us Christ present in the Host and Chalice, really, truly and substantially.

However, precisely because the Eucharistic change is invisible, defining the perimeter within which it occurs is essential. One must be able to identify a point before which what looks like bread and wine is indeed mere bread and wine; and beyond which what still looks like bread and wine is God. The corporal spread over the center of the altar ensures this delineation in space. The corporal is the square linen upon which the Host and Chalice are set at least from the Offertory onward. It is a traditional precaution for newly ordained priests to bind in advance their intention at all their future Masses to consecrate all the hosts and wine present within the edges of the corporal, and only those. This precaution taken once and for all prevents any doubt as to what has been consecrated and what has not. This is particularly relevant if the corporal is small, or if several ciboria are to be consecrated.

The physical posture of the celebrant provides an added delineation. This second delineation regards not space but time. Whereas the celebrant was standing upright before the words of Consecration, he now leans upon the altar, placing his elbows on either side of the corporal, with his head inclined and, only then, utters the sacred words, after which he immediately genuflects. The same occurs for the second formula of Consecration, to change the wine into the Precious Blood. After it, the celebrant resumes his normal posture, standing upright again.

Simultaneously, at the Hanc Igitur prayer, soon before the Consecration, the altar server leaves his usual location at the far right of the lower altar step and comes to kneel close to the celebrant to assist him at the Consecration, walking back to his place at the end of the double Consecration. The bell is rung just before Consecration, adding a sound signal all the more striking as the entire Canon is said in a low voice.

These signs demonstrate that a threshold is about to be crossed. Displayed across space and time, with gestures and sounds, they prompt our souls to adhere in faith to the miraculous change about to occur. Once again, after the Consecration, the eyes of the celebrant, of the server, and of the congregation will still apparently see bread upon the altar and wine inside the Chalice when, in reality, there is no bread and wine left, but only the Body and Blood of Christ with His Soul and Divinity, under the mere externals of bread and wine.

Punctuation

A further sign to mark the threshold to the Consecration is punctuation. Punctuation can be defined as "the nonalphabetical marks, such as the period, comma, colon and brackets, used in writing to separate sentences and their elements and to clarify meaning." The history of punctuation from Greek antiquity to early Christianity and modern Western literature is a fascinating topic, far beyond our present scope. Suffice it to remember that punctuation was originally very sparse. Greek tragedies and even Jewish psalms were meant to be spoken aloud, not read in silence, so that clarity and emphasis depended on the proficiency and inspiration of the actor or worshipper, not on punctuation marks. However, when Christian writings—the Holy Bible, in particular—started being produced in large quantities for study or in the liturgy for users whose native tongue was not Latin, the need for standard disambiguation increased. The rise of printed books strengthened this trend.

Experts could tell how early the punctuation became fixed for the Roman Missal (as to the Latin words, most date from early Christianity, with a few later additions). A copy of an eleventh-century handwritten missal from Spain shows that, even for the Consecration formulas, the use of punctuation and block capitals was not yet standardized. Periods are inserted within sentences where we would have commas and colons instead, and only the second Consecration formula begins with a capital character. Later on, though, in a copy printed in 1515 (and another in Antwerp in 1614), it is moving to see that the punctuation marks are exactly those of the 1962 *versio typica* of the Roman Missal still in use. For what concerns us here, let us point to what looks like an anomaly.

The words of Consecration were first uttered by the Lord Jesus at the Last Supper, speaking in person. After Him, all priests are only quoting His words. The Bible uses direct speech for this. Direct speech inserts punctuation marks — colons in this case — to separate the quoted words from the rest of the text. "And giving thanks, broke, and said: *Take ye, and eat: this is my body, which shall be delivered for you: this do for the commemoration of me.*" (1 Cor. 11:24). The words not in italics are those of the narrator, that is, of St. Paul in this case. The words in italics are those spoken by Christ and here quoted by St. Paul. Obviously, only the words spoken by Christ belong to the formula of Consecration; not those used by St. Paul as narrator. Thus, the words "And giving thanks, broke, and said" are incapable of bringing about transubstantiation. They merely introduce the words of Christ, describing the immediate context in which Christ uttered the words of Consecration.

But the traditional formula of Consecration, in fact, leaves out the first part of Christ's words. Instead of beginning with: "Take ye, and eat," it only starts (and ends) with "For this is my body." Furthermore, the formula ends before the sentence spoken by Christ is completed. Thus, the following words are not part of the first formula of Consecration: "which shall be delivered for you: this do for the commemoration of me." The punctuation anomaly is that the few words of Consecration, "For this is my body," are presented as one single sentence, starting with a capital letter and ending with a period. I call it an anomaly because the words are originally part of a longer sentence spoken by Christ. The anomaly is justified by the fact that the Missal is not the Bible. The words reported in the Bible mean to tell us about Christ. But the same words selected in the Missal are meant to guide our prayer and, at the Consecration, to make Christ truly present.

However, Pope Paul VI suppressed this anomaly when, in his new missal, he extended the first formula of Consecration to make it coincide with the full sentence spoken by Christ. The slightly awkward period (from a linguistic perspective) was gotten rid of. As a consequence, Christ's speech was not interrupted anymore and could be read with more fluidity. This was applied to both Consecration formulas—that is, that of the bread and that of the wine. As stated above, provided the meaning of Christ's words is retained, such changes do not endanger the validity of Consecration. The new formulas undoubtedly achieve this essential aim.

Linguistic continuity within the formula of Consecration is essential, to emphasize its unity. Whatever its length, either shorter (traditional) or longer (modern), the sacred sequence is better uttered, perceived, and meant as one sentence, because the momentous action thus performed is one. The one action is the miraculous change of the substance of bread into that of Christ's flesh (first formula). Soon after, the one action performed is the miraculous change of the substance of wine into that of Christ's Precious Blood (second formula).

For the same reason, discontinuity must clearly be shown between, on the one hand, the narratives immediately preceding and following the words of the Consecration and, on the other hand, the two formulas themselves. Why is discontinuity so important here? Because both the priest celebrant and the congregation must know precisely when St. Paul or Fr. Smith speaks and when Christ the Lord speaks. As explained earlier, the words spoken before the formula of Consecration were first written down by St. Paul and some of the Evangelists (albeit under divine inspiration) and later have been repeated by whichever priest offers Mass. But the words within the formula of Consecration were first spoken by Christ Himself (in Aramaic); and at Holy Mass, they are repeated (in various languages) by the priest, acting as a mere instrument, on behalf of Christ, who is the One truly acting at that moment. In short, everyone must know without doubt when the narration stops and when the action begins. Everyone must know when a mere man speaks and when the God-Man acts. Everyone must distinguish at once between the narrative preceding and the formula following.

Diverse Impact of Words

To help us realize why distinguishing between narration and speech is so important, let us first consider a few examples taken from secular contexts. After this, we will examine what means can help us distinguish safely. Thus, the same words spoken may not have the same impact if the context changes. First, if one morning a judge resolves to exonerate a defendant later that day, he may confide to his colleague: "I will find that midwife not guilty of infanticide." Of course, the midwife is still in custody right after those words are spoken. Second, before entering the courtroom, he may speak aloud the sentence by way of rehearsing: "The hospital staff will be greatly relieved when they hear me say: 'We find the accused not guilty of infanticide.'" Clearly, his words spoken in this private context still make no difference to the legal situation of the accused. Third, when spoken in court that afternoon, they will: the midwife will walk out free. Indirect speech carries no judiciary power in our first example. Direct speech is to no avail in our second example, because the context is private. Only in the third instance does direct speech have judiciary impact.

The higher the authority with which one is endowed, the more important it is to define the context and to clarify the intention. Ambiguity can be fatal, as illustrated in a scenario in a film about the 1954–1962 war in Algeria. Troops ask their captain over the radio what they should do with an enemy just captured on a hill. On hearing the answer "Bring him down!" they shoot the prisoner. The officer only meant that the prisoner should be brought downhill for interrogation. He is later charged with war crime. However, the prisoner does not die a second time when, at the trial, the captain describes the scene: "That afternoon, my men asked me on the radio what they should do with a rebel just captured on the hill. I took the microphone in my hand and distinctly said: 'Bring him down!' " Through those words, an event past is simply recalled.

As a happier example, and moving toward a sacramental context, an engaged couple rehearsing their forthcoming exchange of vows do not become husband and wife by that very fact. The marital bond uniting their souls will come into existence only when they utter the very same words as part of the wedding ceremony.

To summarize, when spoken in a solemn context by persons in authority, certain words carry an objective power whose impact on someone's existence can be highly significant. But the very same words are spoken to no avail or even at risk if the context lacks clarity and if the speaker's intention is not explicit.

The Eucharistic Consecration is a unique case of words causing a change of immense — but undetectable — magnitude. The words of Consecration turn mere bread and wine into God's Body and Blood, but no human being can verify it in this life. The celebrant must therefore be guided by highly explicit signs, stating most clearly the purpose of his action. Furthermore, even though he validly transubstantiates, the Real Presence of Christ that he has brought about will benefit those attending in proportion with their faith. In turn, then, the servers and the congregation must be unambiguously assured that the words spoken by the celebrant are not supposed merely to recall an action past but are meant to effectuate an immediate change. In other words, the mode of speaking must clearly be understood as shifting from narrative to performative. The narration must be known to end, so that the action may begin. Then all can adhere through faith to Christ's invisible presence.

How to achieve this? We need signals. Signs of discontinuity will help identify when the invisible change of transubstantiation is only being introduced (narrative) and when the same invisible change literally occurs (Consecration). Admittedly, such signs would not be needed if Christ appeared visibly on the altar with His Flesh and Blood, as reported in some Eucharistic miracles. If our eyes could tell us when He is not yet there and when He is there, certain precautions would be superfluous. But we don't see the host turn from white to red, nor, for that matter, do we see it growing limbs and taking the bodily shape of the Savior. In fact, we don't see any change at all. We would not taste any change either, or feel any with our fingers, or hear, or smell any before and after Consecration. And yet, the most important event in the world occurs in our presence at every Holy Mass. The Word Incarnate makes Himself truly present on the altar.

Since our physical senses fail to alert us on the change occurring on the altar, we need practical hints to guide our faith through the veil of appearances. Punctuation marks come first among such signs. Looking back at the period I described earlier as an anomaly, in the traditional formula of Consecration, we might appreciate that it helps us precisely as an anomaly. It interrupts the speech of Christ, which is not yet the words of Consecration. Right after the period, a block capital marks the beginning of a new sentence, still part of Christ's speech, but applied this time on a totally different level. For that next sentence is the formula of Consecration, whereby bread becomes the flesh of the God-Man. The same occurs for the second formula, of the wine turned into the Precious Blood. Thus, the period functions as a sign indicating a crucial change of level in the stream of language. The period, so tiny in dimension, flashes in the text like a crucial traffic light regulating the flow of meaning. Like the "On air" sign in a studio when live broadcast begins, the period means: "Attention: narration had just ended. Action has just begun." At this stage, a comparison might help us visualize what is at stake.

Of Salmon and Men

A pitiful sight it was in a wildlife documentary, as hundreds of salmon tried in vain to jump up the powerful stream. As is well known, after years in the ocean, salmon go back to the very river or lake where they were conceived, there to lay their eggs and die. How they find their way back inland and up to remote hill or mountain streams remains a mystery, scientists confess.

In that instance, nature or man had altered the waterfall, so that the stream was simply too strong and steep for the salmon to swim up it. All tried desperately but horribly fell back on the rocks, bouncing with lacerated flesh. Their demise, though, was turned into a feast for the bears and eagles that gathered around the pool and banks literally covered with wounded fish. When environmentalists installed an aqueduct to the side, it saved the animals. New salmon soon found the entrance to the conduit and safely swam their way through to the upper water level.

What about us men? Journeying upstream on hired riverboats is made possible with locks. What happens at a river lock? Large doors open to let boats in. Then the doors shut tightly behind. Water pours in, raising the water inside the compartment up to the upper level, and the boats with it. Other doors open ahead of the boats, which can sail out upstream. You could call the lock a water elevator. Without a lock, boats simply cannot make their way upstream. It might work for strong paddlers on their kayaks against a manageable current, but even those would be defeated, as the salmon were, if they tried to paddle up steep streams, let alone waterfalls.

To refer our analogy to the Consecration at Mass, the difference in levels between the narration before the formula and the action during it is immense. As I said earlier, the first sentence is spoken by mere men, even though as holy as St. Paul, even though inspired by God—while the next one is spoken by Christ, who is God.

The succession of words printed on the page of the missal could be compared to a stream of ink running on paper. While our eyes follow the words during Holy Mass, our minds link one concept to another and, ultimately, our souls posit acts of faith in the invisible change occurring at the Consecration. But as in our previous analogy, the stream is too strong and steep for us to swim up without assistance. Against the compelling evidence provided by our senses, our faith is simply too weak to access the upper level of Christ's invisible presence in the Host and the Chalice. Our eyes, ears, nose, fingers, and tongue tell us that no change has occurred. They rightly attest that what looked like bread and wine a minute earlier still looks like bread and wine. Used to judging of things according to their externals as described by our senses, we spontaneously deduce that there is still only bread and wine on the altar, not the Body and Blood of Christ. However hard our minds and wills try to leap beyond sensorial data, we are incapable of reaching the tranquility of faith unless guided by concrete signs. Without signs, our eyes may read the words, but our minds will not realize the shift from narration to action, and our souls will miss the act of faith.

What are the signs? As seen earlier, three categories of signs come to mind: punctuation marks, physical gestures, and page layout.

Period versus Colon

Let us come back to punctuation marks. They are the more important signs, as they are meant to facilitate the understanding of the words themselves. I called an anomaly the period interrupting Christ's speech right before the traditional Consecration formulas (both italicized by us). That of the bread reads thus: "Take and eat ye all of this. *For this is my body.*" That of the wine reads: "Take and drink ye all of this. *For this is the Chalice of My Blood of the new and eternal Testament, the Mystery of Faith; which shall be shed for you and for many unto the remission of sins.*" At this stage, we can more aptly call this period a most timely signal. It is for us like what the doors into the lock are for the boat or like what the entrance to the conduit is for the salmon. It warns of the difference in levels of signification and allows our journey up.

How is that? The period tells our eyes that a sentence is ending. Our mind understands that the mode of speaking used in that sentence is about to change. It is no more narration. It is about to become action. Our memory then recalls that the Consecration formula will effectuate transubstantiation. Finally, our soul, aided by grace, makes an act of faith in the reality of the sacramental change, despite the remaining externals of bread and wine.

In the new Consecration formulas, a colon replaces the period. Consequently, our eyes can't see the sentence end.

Hence, our mind is likely to assume that the narration goes on, instead of shifting to action mode. Our soul becomes more prone to missing the act of faith in the reality of a change invisible to our eyes and not clearly signaled. We are like a boat thinking itself upon a tranquil stream, when fog conceals from her that Niagara Falls are a hundred yards upstream. There is no way that boat can sail up the fantastic wall of water without being lifted up in a most powerful lock.

One may think the comparison a bit far-fetched, as, after all, the words preceding the Consecration formula are not profane but sacred words as well, by the very fact that they belong to the text of Holy Mass. Furthermore, the worshipper reading those words knows well that he is about to attend the Consecration, so that he is not psychologically unprepared. This is true, for an expert reading a book sitting at his desk. But common experience of the liturgy shows that, once set into a certain understanding of what is happening, our soul requires clear signals to rise to a more demanding mode of signification.

Let us venture yet another very concrete comparison. When a motorcyclist needs a break, his passenger on the back seat can't switch places with him and take the bars unless both stop and dismount. Swapping places while riding is simply impossible, unless both are expert stunt riders in a James Bond film. In ordinary circumstances, no one (let alone their insurer) expects them to swap places until they have come to a halt. Let us call the driver *Narration* and the passenger *Action*. Everyone's assumption is that, as long as the motorcycle moves on, *Narration* is the one holding the bars, not *Action*. Only once the vehicle stops may one envisage that *Action* might come and sit in the front. If we now transpose this example into the field of punctuation, we observe that a shift of linguistic mode from narration to action will require a period. A colon or a semicolon will not suffice unless equivocation is sought. But outside of poetry and playwriting, equivocation is to written information what perilous acrobatics are to motorbike riding: not something expected of average users.

Needless to say, our observations do not apply absolutely, since, in the eleventh-century Spanish missal previously mentioned, punctuation failed to distinguish clearly between narration and action, without impairing the validity of the Consecration. Thus, our reflections aim only at emphasizing the benefit of linguistic clarity enhanced by standardized punctuation, as was secured in the Roman Missal since at least 1515. Liturgical changes are legitimate if they are improvements, not impoverishments. Improvements to the missal answer a need arising from new circumstances, generally heresies.

The first major Eucharistic heresy in the Latin Church was that of Berengarius in the eleventh century in France. He denied the Real Presence of Christ under the externals of bread and wine. In the decades following, as a protestation of faith, in various dioceses and monasteries celebrants started elevating the Sacred Host after the Consecration to present it for adoration to the congregation behind them. It was not long until this initiative was made an official part of the liturgy of Holy Mass. One may assume that improved precision in the layout and punctuation of the Consecration formulas expressed the same desire to state more eloquently the invisible Presence denied by the heresiarch. Such a need only increased when the Protestant revolt broke out in the sixteenth century.

Are We Stronger Than Our Forefathers?

We Eucharistic worshippers in the third millennium are no less in need of liturgical signs to help our faith than our twelfth-century forefathers. In fact, so many philosophical and theological errors have sprung up in the modern era, undermining or directly negating Christ's Real Presence, that our need for clear liturgical affirmation is greater than ever. Deprived of clear signs, among which punctuation marks hold pride of place, our soul will more or less consciously interpret as symbolic the divine presence, judging by our physical senses. Who will say that faith in the reality of the substantial change at Mass is easy and ever complete? Since the loving intensity of that faith is the very criterion of our merit in attending Holy Mass and of the fruit received thereof, is it not of the utmost importance that we should examine what facilitates such faith and what hinders it?

As such, is not the difference spectacular between, on the one hand, St. Paul or Fr. Smith narrating the Eucharistic institution at the Last Supper and, on the other hand, the God-Man, Christ Himself, changing the substance of bread into that of His Body and, soon after, the substance of wine into that of His Blood? The level of understanding of a soul who fails to discern Christ's Body and Blood after Consecration is abysmally lower than that of a faithful soul confessing the Real Presence — just like the respective positions of our first boat down before Niagara Falls and of another boat hypothetically lifted up and speeding upstream with full power.

Furthermore, the Eucharistic faith of priests is no less vulnerable than that of their flock. If the laity can find it hard to believe that Christ's Real Presence occurs at the Consecration, priests do not have it any easier. In reference to our previous analogy, priests as well must swim upstream. Leading the way for the people they serve, priests must leave sensorial data behind and reach the upper water level, that of faith. Failing that, they die spiritually. A tragic illustration could be the original poster of the celebrated 1986 film *The Mission*, about Jesuit missionaries in eighteenth-century Paraguay. The image shows a bare-chested man tied upon a cross (a martyred priest, in this instance), falling down a gigantic waterfall. May God preserve priests from such a catastrophic Eucharistic downfall, from divine faith to mere senses! It takes hard work, humility, and perseverance for priests to ascend to the upper level and there to communicate to souls the true Body and Blood of God. But with adequate liturgical signs, sound theology, and the grace of God, this narrow path can be walked, following in the footsteps of billions of Catholics.

Swimming upstream toward the Eucharistic Christ is more than an analogy. A torrent of grace is truly flowing from above us, although invisibly. On Easter morning, Holy Mother Church puts the following words on our lips at the Vidi Aquam preceding Holy Mass: "I saw water coming out from the temple, from the right side, alleluia." While we breathe on earth, we are meant to travel in spirit toward the Sacred Heart, whence springs the salvific stream solemnly witnessed by St. John: "One of the soldiers with a spear opened his side, and immediately there came out blood and water. And he that saw it, hath given testimony, and his testimony is true. And he knoweth that he saith true; that you also may believe" (John 19:34–35). The downstream current flows from Christ's Heart, pierced for our sins, and runs toward us, His redeemed children and members. It calls for a response. Our response consists in progressing upstream, until we reach the safety of His Heart and dwell in It forever: "And I, if I be lifted up from the earth, will draw all things to myself" (John 12:32); and "Come to me, all you that labour, and are burdened, and I will refresh you. Take up my yoke upon you, and learn of me, because I am meek, and humble of heart: and you shall find rest to your souls" (Matt. 11:28-29).

Bearing in mind these historical and spiritual considerations, let us return to our literal examination of the missal. As mentioned above, the words of the two Consecration formulas remained unchanged from the earliest times in Church history. But more strikingly, the period before and after the two formulas, as well as the capital letter at the beginning of each of them, are attested from at least 1515—that is, from the early printed versions of the Roman Missal. This applies to the altar missal used by the celebrant at Mass but not so continuously to the hand missals of the faithful. Strangely, while those normally display the correct punctuation for the Latin original, they fail to replicate it for the English translation on the opposite page, where the period is often replaced by a colon or a comma. The same occurs even in the Latin on some altar cards (i.e., the main prayers of Mass framed separately and set on the altar during Holy Mass for the celebrant's convenience). One would wish those discrepancies to be corrected, so that vernacular translations and altar cards should faithfully replicate the official punctuation displayed in the altar missal. However, the layout and punctuation truly normative are those of the altar missal, which is the liturgical volume used to offer the Holy Sacrifice. It is sufficient to notice again and marvel at its unchanged punctuation from the early days of the print era.

Such continuity ended in 1969 with the new missal of Pope Paul VI. In it, the official Latin text on the altar missal entails extended Consecration formulas. The *editio typica* 2002 begins each formula with a capital letter. The 2010 English edition gives the entire Consecration formulas in capital letters, which better indicates the performative function of the formulas, in conformity with the *Constitution Missale Romanum*. But in either case, both missals introduce the formulas with a colon, instead of the traditional period. Linguistically speaking then, the formulas may appear to belong to the narration preceding.

This impression increases when too short a pause is made after the narrative clause ends, before speaking the Consecration formula and when the tone of voice does not differ (in volume, intonation, and slowness) from the one used for the narration preceding. Those issues do not apply to the traditional formulas, since they are spoken in a low voice, like the entire Canon of the Mass. In this case, the congregation is guided by the punctuation in their Latin hand missal. Changing the period to a colon (or to a comma, as in certain English versions of the traditional missal), makes it more difficult to realize that the narration stops and that the action begins. The mind tends to continue to read as narration what is an action. Unless one has received precise catechetical explanation as to what truly happens at Holy Mass, one may assume that Christ's presence in the Host and Chalice is a vivid memory recalled and should not to be taken literally. Just as the event of the Institution of Mass in Jerusalem, narrated by the celebrant, belongs to the past—so the presence of Christ might be interpreted as mere commemoration.

Genuflections

Let us examine the rationale explaining the 1969 changes of the Consecration formulas. Pope Paul VI's constitution *Missale Romanum*, presenting the main changes and guiding principles for the new Missal, stated:

> Also to be eliminated are "elements which, with the passage of time, came to be duplicated, or were added with but little advantage," above all in the rites of offering the bread and wine, and in those of the breaking of the bread and of communion.

Duplications then were to be eliminated, in particular those in close connection with the Host.

This principle was duly implemented as regards the genuflections. Traditionally, the celebrant would genuflect immediately after consecrating the Host and again right after consecrating the Precious Blood. He would then rise, elevate the Host, and genuflect again; the same for the Chalice. The new Missal suppressed both first genuflections. The rubric of the traditional missal clearly stated the meaning of the first genuflection: to adore. The gesture stressed the fact that no sooner had the celebrant uttered the sacred formula of Consecration than Christ was truly present. The objectiveness of the divine presence that had just occurred called for immediate acknowledgment by the celebrant, even before anyone else would actually see the host.

Retaining only the second genuflection could lead some of the faithful to assume that what the celebrant holds in his hands becomes worthy of adoration only after the people have assented to the presence in the Host shown them at the elevation.

The first genuflection, on the contrary, affirmed that Christ's presence in no way depends on the faith of those attending but occurs by the very power of the sacrament validly performed by the priest. Since the first genuflection before the elevation was suppressed, it must have been understood by the authors of the new missal as a "useless repetition." One might argue that, by definition, the *first* genuflection is not a repetition since it is initial; but the *second* is, so that in good logic, the second genuflection after the elevation should have been suppressed, not the first one after Consecration. However, at least as regards genuflections, the principle laid down by Pope Paul VI can be invoked to explain the changes. Let us now examine another physical posture supporting our Eucharistic faith.

The Yogi, the Iroquois, and the Deaf

Considering a familiar gesture from a totally different angle can deepen our understanding of it. Therefore, our reader is requested to permit the following incursion into deep pagan territory for the sake of illustrating (not condoning). Not infrequently, now, yoga lessons are advertised in Catholic parishes and monasteries. The purpose is "to teach well-being." If we dare mention what we have cautiously gleaned on the Internet about yoga, the best-known position of hands or "mudra" is called "gyan." It plainly consists in joining the tips of both the forefingers and thumbs while the other fingers remain straight. Allegedly, this posture has brought "spiritual energy and peace to yogis for thousands years, stimulating the gland controlling our metabolism, improving memory and fostering clarity of mind"—no less! Performing "gyan" for half an hour daily is recommended by Eastern "sages."

Ego Eimi—It Is I

One wonders if, on the Far Western side of the world, the ferocious Iroquois had guessed the power accrued from the "gyan" posture and tried to counter it. Mutilating fingers was a torture they particularly enjoyed inflicting. Although lay prisoners as well as clerics were subjected to it, one of their priest victims is particularly memorable. The Jesuit missionary St. Isaac Jogues was a deeply spiritual man. The Iroquois thought him a sorcerer. In 1642, Iroquois spies or converts watching him say Mass in his forest hut or clearing would have been struck by the mysterious rites performed by the priest at the makeshift altar.

In particular, once the climax of the sacred action was reached, they would have noticed that his thumbs and fore-fingers remained joined, after the rubric prescribing that the celebrant: "does not disjoin his thumbs and index fingers up to the ablution of the fingers after the Communion, except when he must touch or handle the consecrated Host." While they ignored the reason for this conspicuous gesture, the natives would have understood its intrinsic connection with the numinous power produced by the Eucharistic rite. The Iroquois cut off the priest's left thumb and forefinger, and several other fingers on his right hand. Back in Europe, St, Isaac Jogues was granted by Pope Urban VIII special permission to continue offering Holy Mass, as Church law then forbade performing the sacred action with missing fingers.

The traditional missal still in force describes as follows the position of the celebrant's fingers from the Consecration onward:

And holding his own Host with his thumbs and index fingers, he says: HOC EST ENIM CORPUS MEUM.

When this has been said, the Celebrant, holding the Host between his afore-mentioned thumbs and index fingers upon the Altar, with the remaining fingers of his hands extended, and at the same time joined, genuflecting, he adores It. Then he arises, and as much as he can comfortably do, elevates the Host in the air, and directing his eyes toward It (which is also done during the elevation of the Chalice), shows It reverently to the people, for their adoration. And soon he reverently replaces It upon the Corporal with his right hand only, in the same place from which he raised It, and without interruption. *He does not disjoin his thumbs and index fingers up to the ablution of the fingers after the Communion, except when he must touch or handle the consecrated Host.*"

The reason for this posture is obviously not to capture dubious energies, as yogis would have it—God forbid! Rather, the purpose is to prevent any sacred fragment of consecrated Host, possibly adhering to the tips of the celebrant's four digits, from being dropped inadvertently. This would otherwise happen when holding the stem of the chalice or turning the pages of the missal with disjoined forefingers and thumbs. The joined thumbs and forefingers are a very powerful liturgical sign, strengthening the faith of the celebrant and the congregation in the reality of Christ's presence, even in Eucharistic fragments. It is a very simple and costless protection of the Blessed Sacrament as well as a witness to the Savior's invisible presence.

In the new missal, this position of the celebrant's fingers is no longer prescribed or even mentioned. It must have been considered one of those redundant "elements which, with the passage of time, came to be duplicated, or were added with but little advantage." Some priests adopt it, though, when using the new missal, since it is not forbidden. But they know that this gesture may raise some eyebrows among their congregation and possibly their colleagues. Surely, with the right explanation, every lover of the Eucharist would support this simple sign of reverence. Or would it not be awkward if a gesture praised by some Catholics in the context of pagan spiritualities became unwelcome when observed by devout celebrants at the altar?

Generally speaking, any Catholic would agree that gestures convey meaning. For example, a dedicated priest once learned sign language for the benefit of a deaf parishioner. He felt sorry for that person, whom he assumed could not participate fully in the Mass (the new missal was used). That priest would not have taken the trouble to learn sign language unless he believed that the position of his hands communicated meaningful information, although not spoken. Advertisers and public speakers know well that verbal communication accounts only for the smaller part of the information we send and receive. Long before the use of body language, of colors, of shapes, and of sounds was theorized, Holy Mother Church was using all those nonverbal resources in her liturgy to feed the souls of her children with the truths of faith.

In American Sign Language, the letter "F" is expressed by joining the tips of the thumb and forefinger while keeping the three other fingers extended. Hundreds of words begin with "F," some more evocative than others, such as "flower," "fire," "feather," and "father." None better than "faith" however applies to the posture of the celebrant's hands after consecrating Christ's Body in a traditional Holy Mass. If hearing-impaired worshippers interpreted it in that way, their handicap would by no means hinder their deep participation in the Mystery of Faith occurring on the altar at the hands of the priest. On equal footing with all other worshippers during the silent Canon of the Mass, they would have before their eyes the "F"-shaped hands of the priest, a soundless but all-the-more-expressive witness to the necessity of faith in Christ's sacrificial presence. At shoulder height on either side of the ornate chasuble seen from behind, the "faith"-shaped hands of the priest speak more eloquently than words.

Worshippers would read the contrast between the joined and extended fingers on either hand as an ultimate call to discerning in faith between profane and sacred. This distinction applies from broader to narrower—between street and church, between church nave and sanctuary, between sanctuary floor and altar, between altar cloth and corporal, between the servers' bare hands and the priest's anointed palms, between the corporal and the Sacred Species. This gradual focusing culminates in the setting aside of the thumb and forefinger of both hands. Why? Because they have touched God. They are touching God, either while holding the Sacred Host, or simply because fragments of the Host might still adhere to their tips. Until rinsed with wine and water after Communion and dried with the linen purificator, those four digits are to touch nothing but God's Sacred Body.

Let the other six fingers turn the tabs of the missal pages and seize the chalice stem (along which the knob is traditionally set halfway between the foot and the cup to provide a secure grasp between the index finger and the major fingers).

No part of the human body can ever be more eloquently withdrawn from profane use than these four first digits are, from the Consecration until the ablutions. Joining the tips of those digits is the visual apex of liturgical communication. In that context, truly the priestly gesture is loaded with the highest possible meaning. What it expresses is far more real than a symbol, because those two pairs of digits are joined through practical faith in God's immediate presence at their tips. They provide the strongest protection for our Eucharistic faith.

Would that all men read this sign! O Yogis, the hand posture you praise without knowing its true meaning, this we reveal to you. O Iroquois, the rite you tried to suppress (confessing its power) fosters your greatest good, if you will believe. O modern men, if you boast of having entered the *digital* era, the Church's tradition welcomes you in it, as the four *digits* of her priests maintain this sacred posture, connecting you and us with the earliest times of faith. O credulous ones who hope that your crossed fingers will secure luck: learn that God's Providence, which governs everything, is never more propitious than when at the altar the priest's thumbs and index fingers join in faith.

We can't call this posture "gyan," can we? It demands a better name from us Catholics. We could call it "padlock," since, when our priests' forefingers reaches their thumbs, our faith in our Savior's presence among us His people is iron fastened. But "padlock" fails to express the dynamic and collective nature of the sacred action.

Half a mile across town, north of the railway station, a rather nice-looking church has been turned into an indoor climbing wall. This unfortunate sign of the times may help illustrate our purpose. Holy Mass is about ascending Mount Golgotha in spirit. We follow the lead climber up the steep wall of faith, toward the summit of sacrifice. We are safe once he has pushed the rope through the "carabiner," the metal loop that secures the roped climbers. The position of the celebrant's four digits may be compared to a carabiner. His joined digits figure twin rings. If they were of aluminum, as for actual climbing, they could not haul the weight of more than a few dozen men. But those liturgical "carabiners" are wrought in a stronger metal called *faith*, and thus they can carry up thousands, even millions, of souls. Thankfully, if ever the lead climber stalled or slipped, those loops of faith might prevent his own downfall. Please God and through His grace, as the priest's index fingers meet his thumbs after the Consecration, he safely leads our souls into the mystery of faith, to victory above. That is our goal, where the Savior calls us, with Mary and John, with Magdalene and Longinus, and with all humanity redeemed.

Dotty about a Dot

"Useless duplications and additions" were to be suppressed from the new missal. We just saw this principle applied to several gestures immediately connected with the Consecration formulas. Surprisingly, the same principle was contradicted, not as regards gestures, such as genuflections or the position of fingers, but with punctuation. Where, for at least 450 years, there was one period before the Consecration, marking the beginning of each Consecration formula, a colon was put instead.

Let us visualize this. Concretely, the single ink dot on the page at that place in the text was doubled. What is a colon, but a dot added above another dot? Thus, where there was one dot, a second dot was added. What improvement this change was meant to bring about is unclear. It is thus questionable according to the Vatican II Constitution on the Liturgy: "There must be no innovations unless the good of the Church genuinely and certainly requires them."[32] The motive for suppressing the period before Consecration must have been very serious indeed.

Some readers may wonder why we are coming back to that dot. Should we not forget that ink speck and move on? Lady Macbeth's famous quote might even spring to mind: "Out, damned spot!" Admittedly, a dot is but a dot. But the more precious or dangerous its context, the deeper the justification needed to alter it. Let us consider a few concrete examples. If a music publisher arbitrarily inserted a dot after a note on the score of, let us say, Mozart's *Missa Solemnis in C major*, experts would protest against this alteration of the tempo assigned by the composer. Admittedly, Catholicism and its liturgy are living realities susceptible to change, unlike the Mozart corpus, which is diversely performed but not to be altered. Let us repeat that changes in the liturgy are not the issue, but their purposes and effects are, and these must bring improvement.

To remain in the domain of fine arts, only painter Claude Monet, the father of Impressionism, could say whether a copyist had painted one dot too many on a reproduction of his famous painting *Impression, Sunrise*. We the public would be at a loss to find out. And what of Georges Seurat, who

---

[32] Second Vatican Council, Constitution on the Liturgy *Sacrosanctum Concilium* (December 4, 1963), no. 23.

invented *pointillism*, a painting method consisting in a juxta-position of colored dots, prefiguring the pixels in our digital pictures? Again we see that dots matter to produce an effect, but their number and positioning can be subjective, escaping the sagacity of average amateurs.

In the domain of techniques, though, such as modern communication, everyone immediately recognizes that one single dot makes a huge difference. Take an e-mail address for instance: a single dot typed in the wrong place will prevent the sending of a message. The same would apply to a website address: a mere dot mistyped will prevent access to the wealth of information awaiting us, as the webpage simply won't open. Similarly, an electronic accounting sheet will not tolerate a single dot misplaced in the figure of the least transaction, as the entire sum would be altered.

In reference to these examples, we can ponder the impact of punctuation changes affecting liturgical art, even of a single dot. We admit the importance of artistic integrity, altered through the addition of one dot. We have experienced the stubbornness of modern tools that won't obey us if we add but one dot in the wrong place. It would be surprising if, as Catholics, we thought that the addition of one dot before the Consecration formula were meaningless. Is not Holy Mass the most important "communication" of all: that of divine grace? Does it not demand the most exact accounting: that of the Precious Blood shed for us unto the last drop? Does it not deserve a consideration of its every detail greater than all the works of art in the world, as God is the One inspir-ing that work?

The closer to the center, the heavier the duty to justify an alteration, by stating in what objective improvement it resulted. Let us have recourse to imagination again. If, early one morning, Bob changes the combination on his bicycle padlock, no one should object or even ask him for an explanation. This change concerns only Bob. Once arrived at his workplace — a power station for instance — if Bob changes the combination to disable the surveillance cameras, one expects a higher authority to check and authorize Bob's action. Later on, Bob becomes director of the power station. What, then, if he alters the access code to the nuclear reactor? The consequence could obviously be much more serious. And yet, when one considers the magnitude of the power produced, nuclear fission in a reactor is a mere trifle compared with the reenactment of the sacrifice of Calvary and the occurring of God's Real Presence.

My contention, then, is that turning the period into a colon immediately before the Consecration formula makes it less obvious that transubstantiation is taking place and that Christ's presence occurs not symbolically but in reality. I fail to see what improvement this alteration, affecting the immediate access to the sacramental "reactor" of the Church, has brought about.

Moreover, this change was not the only one. I explained earlier the suppression of the first genuflection after consecrating the Body and Blood of Christ. A further change affected specifically the second formula, that of the Consecration of the Precious Blood. The traditional formula consisted in a single sentence. The new one is longer, comprising two sentences. Where there was one single sentence, another sentence was added. It lessens the linguistic unity of the formula whereby, to one idea or action, corresponds one sentence. But its most profound alteration I will now describe.

Faith and Memory

For a thousand years at least, the words *Mysterium Fidei*, meaning "Mystery of faith," were part of the formula of Consecration of the Precious Blood. On November 29, 1209, Pope Innocent III was referring to a long-established fact when he stated:

> The expression "Mystery of faith" is used, because here what is believed differs from what is seen, and what is seen differs from what is believed. For what is seen is the appearance of bread and wine and what is believed is the reality of the flesh and blood of Christ and the power of unity and love.... We believe that the apostles have received from Christ the words of the formula found in the Canon, and their successors have received them from the apostles.[33]

In the new missal, the words *Mysterium Fidei* were taken out of the formula and were instead inserted *after* the formula. In *Missale Romanum*, Pope Paul VI's presentation of the new missal quoted above, he wrote: "The words MYSTERIUM FIDEI, taken from the context of the words of Christ the Lord, and said by the priest, serve as an introduction to the acclamation of the faithful." At the same time, the reference to "memory" that followed immediately after the traditional formula was made part of the new formula, using the words: "Do this in memory of me" (in Latin: *Hoc facite in meam commemorationem*). In the new missal, one expression replaced the other. "Mystery of faith" was taken out of the formula and inserted right after it. Instead, the word "memory" was

---

[33] Pope Innocent III, letter to Archbishop John of Lyons.

taken from its place after the traditional formula and inserted within the new formula. In short, "memory" and "faith" were swapped.

Let us reflect on the meaning of the expressions. In the traditional formula, "Mystery of faith" refers to the transubstantiation just occurring. It provides the key to access the treasure. What is that key? That key is faith in the Real Presence, unlocking the treasure of Christ's merits. Faith is the knowledge of realities beyond the very limited range of our physical senses. In this instance, the object of faith is the true presence of Christ's Precious Blood under the externals of wine. Coming in the second formula, after the first Consecration of the bread into the Body of Christ, the words "Mystery of faith" apply also to the presence of Christ in the host, under the externals of bread. "Mystery of faith" is thus a manifesto enshrined in the very center of the formula, stating that faith is the necessary condition for accessing the presence of Christ in the Holy Eucharist.

Our faith by no means *causes* the presence. As mentioned earlier concerning the first genuflection, regardless of our faith, the formula uttered by the priest does effect the transubstantiation. Our faith is required, then, not to cause the presence but to benefit from it. Without faith, we cannot relate to the Holy Eucharist. It profits us nothing. Even worse, if for want of faith we failed to discern Christ's presence in the consecrated Host and Chalice, receiving the Holy Eucharist would mean our condemnation, as St. Paul warned the early Christians.

What is the meaning of the other expression, "Do this in memory of me," inserted into the new formula for the Consecration of the wine into the Precious Blood? As we know, in the New Testament, only Sts. Luke, Mark, Matthew, and Paul mention the Institution of the Eucharist. St. John does not refer to it. Sts. Mark and Matthew make no mention of "memory" or "remembrance" for either Consecration. St. Luke and St. Paul are the only two who mention the words "Do this in memory of me."

St. Paul is the only one who mentions the word "memory" after the *second* Consecration formula. But the words of Christ that St. Paul then reports are not those inserted in the new Consecration formula. Instead, St. Paul wrote: "Every time you shall do these things, you will do them in memory of me" (see 1 Cor. 11:25). That sentence immediately follows the second Consecration formula in the traditional missal, just as St. Paul gave it in his epistle. The same sentence was deleted from the new missal, whether in or near the formulas of Consecration. The sentence inserted in the new formula for the Consecration of the wine into the Precious Blood is given both by St. Luke and St. Paul after the *first* Consecration formula: that of the bread into Christ's Body. Thus, in the new missal, St. Paul's quotation after the *second* Consecration was deleted, and his or St Luke's quotation after the *first* Consecration was inserted instead. The new missal reverses the order of the biblical narrative. The Church has the authority to make such changes. But the principle invoked cannot be that of a more literal fidelity to Scriptures.

The words "Do this in memory of me," spoken by the Lord Jesus at the Last Supper, empowered the Apostles and their successors to offer the Eucharistic sacrifice, following His example. On September 17, 1562, the Council of Trent defined that, when speaking those words, Christ ordained the Apostles priests: "If any one saith, that by those words, Do this for the commemoration of me [Luke 22:19; 1 Cor. 11:24], Christ did not institute the Apostles priests; or, did not ordain that they and other priests should offer his own body and blood: let him be anathema."[34] It is a dogmatic truth, then, that those words constitute the formula of the first priestly ordination ever performed. The new missal inserts the formula of priestly ordination into the formula of Eucharistic Consecration. One should bear in mind that both sacraments are mutually connected but distinct: the priesthood in one case; the Holy Eucharist in the other case. The sacrament of the Holy Eucharist is necessary to the life of the Church, but it is also conditioned by the sacrament of Holy Orders: no Church without the Eucharist—no Holy Eucharist without priests. Since few people know about the dogmatic definition of Trent just mentioned, however, the majority will not perceive the expression "Do this in memory of me" as affirming the distinctive essence of the ministerial priesthood.

The words "Do this in memory of me" inserted in the new Consecration formula of the wine into the Precious Blood emphasize the word "memory." By definition, "memory" refers to things past. The implication is that things are not truly present in the moment when they are remembered. With tenderness, a mother can tell her grown-up son that she remembers when he first walked. Now a grown man, the son is present in the room as she speaks, but his first steps are long gone. Putting this emphasis on memory in the formula of Consecration does not deny the presence of Christ in the sacrament. But it brings in a risk of distraction, as it

---

[34] Session 22, chap. 9, canon 2, on the Sacrifice of the Mass.

leads the mind to focus on the first occurrence of Christ's Eucharistic presence, at the first Consecration in Jerusalem, in the year 33. It would seem more helpful to focus on the reality of the presence immediately and actually occurring, in whichever church or chapel a priest is offering Mass, in whichever country and time.

During Holy Mass, one does not have the time to unfold the full meaning of the two expressions "Mystery of faith" and "Do this in memory of me," as we have just done. Rather, what the mind will instinctively grasp is that, in the modern formula of Consecration, one is asked to remember something past; whereas in the traditional formula, one is meant to believe in someone present. Angels are pure spirits who see things intuitively without the mediation of bodily senses. Unlike theirs, the human mind finds it difficult to affirm that something is present when one's physical senses fail to detect it. Judging by our senses is natural to our minds. It is our minds' default setting. On the contrary, judging by faith is arduous. According to our human nature, we are prone to explain away as a cherished and powerful *memory* a presence that we may neither deny nor see, hear, or touch. Emphasizing the word "memory" at the crucial moment of Consecration exposes those among us who are neither angels nor experts to the risk of an increasingly spiritual understanding of Christ's presence in the Eucharist.

When reading the new formula in the light of the traditional one, it appears that swapping faith with memory leads to swap believing with recalling, and present with past. Unless one is very well catechized, the risk is not small that one's understanding of Christ's presence will shift gradually from physical to spiritual; from real to symbolic; from objective to subjective. Such was not Pope Paul VI's intention, when on September 3, 1965, only a few years before promulgating his new missal, he signed *Mysterium Fidei*, a full encyclical on the absolute preeminence of Christ's Real Presence in the Eucharist. Only a few months before decreeing the radical changes in the missal through the Constitution *Missale Romanum* (April 3, 1969), Pope Paul VI stated again most clearly the Catholic truth on the Real Presence. This occurred on January 10, 1969 in *Saluberrimum Sacramentum Eucharistiae*, a letter from the pope to the superior general of the Priests of the Blessed Sacrament on worship of the Eucharist outside Holy Mass.

I now quote its first paragraph:

> The most salutary sacrament of the Eucharist stands as the centre of the Church's life because it contains really, truly, and substantially the author of grace himself. Therefore it takes hold of the minds of believers in such a way that they understand, not by force of elaborate argument but by a kind of insight into the reality, that they should offer to this sacrament the worship of adoration. The effect of this exercise of worship is the expression and increase of the virtue of religion by which the believing spirit acknowledges its all-transcending creator and his lordship and strives for the attitude of submissive reverence proper to the creature. This adoration is shown even through the body, which is offered as a "living sacrifice, holy and acceptable to God." As St. Thomas Aquinas writes, "In all acts of worship what is exterior is related to what is interior as to the more important element. Therefore exterior adoration takes place because of the interior,

namely, in order that the signs of humility that we manifest through the body may stir our affections to subject themselves to God."

But very few read *Mysterium Fidei*, and who has heard of *Saluberrimum Sacramentum Eucharistiae*? Meanwhile, all those attending the Pauline Mass hear the word "memory" emphasized in the Consecration formula and the word "faith" mentioned only outside the same formula. For the reasons explained earlier, this swap makes it more difficult to discern the true presence of Christ.

Discerning the Body

This will be the last point in our study of the Consecration formulas. It refers to the scriptural quotes in the missal as a whole, rather than to the Consecration formulas specifically. But it is relevant to our topic inasmuch as it bears upon the sacrificial purpose of the Holy Eucharist, and upon the duty to discern Christ's presence beneath the externals of bread and wine.

St. Paul warns us:

> Whosoever shall eat this bread, or drink of the chalice of the Lord unworthily, shall be guilty of the body and the blood of the Lord. But let a man prove himself; and so let him eat of that bread, and drink of the chalice. For he that eateth and drinketh unworthily, eateth and drinketh judgment to himself, not discerning the body of the Lord. (1 Cor. 11:27-29)

Catholics who read their Bibles at home might be familiar with this warning by St. Paul, but none can hear or read it at

Holy Mass, unfortunately. Why is that? Because the Apostle's timely warning was taken out of the new missal. These verses were deleted, as was the one a couple of lines earlier, as I have just explained: "Every time you shall do these things, you will do them in memory of me" (see 1 Cor 11:25).

The traditional missal quotes St. Paul's momentous words on numerous occasions. Every Maundy Thursday and Corpus Christi, St. Paul's warning is read. Every Thursday in the year when no feast or privileged occasion takes precedence, St. Paul's warning can be heard in the Votive Mass of the Blessed Sacrament. Moreover, that very quote is reiterated within the same votive Mass. It is given in full as the Epistle and again selectively as the Communion antiphon. (In addition, it is read on another two occasions in the traditional breviary in the ninth reading of *Tenebrae* on Maundy Thursday and the third reading of Matins on Corpus Christi.)

The apostolic warning against sacrilegious reception of Christ's Body was deemed so salutary that it became enshrined in the third prayer of the celebrant before his own Communion: "Perceptio corporis tui ... — Let the receiving of Thy Body, O Lord Jesus Christ, which I presume to receive, though unworthy, turn not unto me for judgment and condemnation ..." This prayer was first seen in the ninth century and has been a part of the Mass since the tenth century. Thankfully, it was retained in Paul VI's new missal, but only as a second option.[35] The new missal, however, does not offer the choice until *after* the celebrant has read the first (optional) prayer. Before that first prayer, the rubric states: "Then the priest, with hands joined, says quietly: [the

[35] See GIRM 268.

first prayer follows]". To offer a real choice, the alternative should have been indicated earlier, for instance: "Then the priest, with hands joined, says quietly *one of the two following* prayers." But the word "or" appears on the page only *after* the first prayer — that is, too late. Consequently, the priest is unlikely to "annul" the prayer he has just read as he was told. Instead, he may well skip the one offered further down, having by then remembered that it is not compulsory.

As a result, it is perfectly licit for a celebrant never in his life to use that prayer when offering Mass. This deprives the priest of a most salutary warning against unworthy Communion. That third prayer is obligatory in the traditional Missal, as a powerful encouragement to confess Christ's presence at this very last moment before consuming the Sacred Host. By consequence, it is also a loving incentive for the priest to be absolved beforehand from any grave sin, if ever needed.

The traditional missal provided yet a further warning against sacrilegious Communion in the "Lauda Sion," the celebrated sequence of Corpus Christi. In that beautiful poem, St. Thomas Aquinas reminded his fellow Catholics that: "The good receive Him, the bad receive Him, but with what unequal consequences of life or death. It is death to the unworthy, life to the worthy: behold then of a like reception, how unlike may be the result!" Taken out of the new missal, the "Lauda Sion" was retained in the lectionary only as an option, as the rubric states: "The optional sequence (Lauda Sion) is intended to be sung; otherwise it is better omitted. The shorter version (Ecce Panis) begins at the asterisk." That "shorter version" (comprising two strophes out of twelve, or four out of twenty-four) omits the strophes with the warning quoted above. Some lectionaries don't have the "Lauda Sion" printed on the page for the Solemnity of Corpus Christi but refer the celebrant to the thin "Sequences" section toward the end of the thick volume. It makes saying the optional "Lauda Sion" less convenient, hence less likely.

Thus, on the very feast of the Eucharist, this important reminder on the conditions for a fruitful Communion can be totally ignored. It is one less opportunity for the congregation and the celebrant to grow in reverential love for the Eucharistic Body of Christ. Such impoverishment is not remedied by greater emphasis on the Precious Blood, since the feast of the Most Precious Blood on July 1 was taken out of the new calendar.

But let us return to St. Paul's letter. Bearing in mind the principle examined earlier in Pope Paul VI's Constitution on the new Roman Missal—namely, to suppress repetitions—especially when connected with the Eucharist, one might have expected to see several of those occurrences of chapter 11 in St. Paul's First Letter to the Corinthians being deleted from the new missal.

What was unexpected was for each and all occurrences of 1 Corinthians 11:20-22 and 27-32 to disappear from the missal. So it happened, nevertheless. To the best of our knowledge, in Pope Paul VI's new missal, St. Paul's warning does not occur one single time. This is all the more striking as it flatly contradicts another principle set by the constitution on the new missal: "A more representative portion of the Holy Scriptures will be read to the people." The traditional missal was found too selective in its scriptural quotes. This led to the unprecedented change from a one-year cycle of readings (whose structure had remained the same for over a millennium) to a three-year cycle. In that perspective, the systematic suppression of each and all occurrences of St. Paul's solemn call to Eucharistic discernment is even less understandable. The traditional missal cannot at the same time be found wanting in scriptural quotes and purged from the very verses it insisted upon, reiterating them on so many occasions, as we just saw.

These quotes from 1 Corinthians 11 were extremely helpful to fortify our Eucharistic faith about two essential truths. The first truth is that Holy Mass is a sacrifice, to be clearly distinguished from a mere meal:

> When you come therefore into one place, it is not now to eat the Lord's supper. For every one taketh before his own supper to eat. And one indeed is hungry and another is drunk. What, have you not houses to eat and to drink in? Or despise ye the church of God and put them to shame that have not? What shall I say to you? Do I praise you? In this I praise you not. (1 Cor. 11:20-22)

The second truth is the objective reality of Christ's bodily presence under the externals of bread and wine. No one must receive without discerning this Real Presence in faith, thus excluding any symbolic or merely spiritual interpretation of the presence. Those failing to discern, condemn themselves:

> Therefore, whosoever shall eat this bread, or drink the chalice of the Lord unworthily, shall be guilty of the body and the blood of the Lord. But let a man prove himself; and so let him eat of that bread and drink of the chalice. For he that eateth and drinketh unworthily eateth and drinketh judgment to himself, not

discerning the body of the Lord. Therefore are there many infirm and weak among you: and many sleep. But if we would judge ourselves, we should not be judged. But whilst we are judged, we are chastised by the Lord, that we be not condemned with this world. (1 Cor. 11:27–32)

Noticeably, 1 Corinthians 11:26, that is, the verse preceding the quote deleted from the traditional missal, was inserted in the new missal immediately after the words "Mystery of faith." Thus, St. Paul's verse 26 reads: "For as often as you shall eat this bread, and drink the chalice, you shall shew the death of the Lord, until he come." The text of the new missal transposes St. Paul's words to the first person plural, as if the Christians of Corinth were now the ones speaking to Christ: "When we eat this Bread and drink this Cup, we proclaim your Death, O Lord, until you come again." The traditional missal quoted St. Paul's verse 25 immediately after the second Consecration formula: "This do ye, as often as you shall drink, for the commemoration of me." It skipped verse 26 but later quoted verse 27 and following (four times over the year, as explained earlier). In striking contrast, the new missal does the exact opposite. It suppresses verse 25; it brings in verse 26; and deletes every mention of verses 27 and following.

Tracing those many alterations in the new formulas of Consecration is a bit strenuous, admittedly. The reward for our exertions however is a better familiarity with the spiritual and theological implications of such changes. Raising liturgical awareness benefits us if it leads us to value more greatly the ritual signs given us by Holy Mother Church to strengthen our faith and thus, to unite us with God.

Conclusion

Reverently considering the words, layout, gestures, and punctuation of the two Consecration formulas helps us to realize better the connection between liturgical form and contents. Our examination shows how the sacrificial nature of Holy Mass and the objective reality of Christ's presence under the externals of bread and wine are diversely expressed in the current traditional Roman missal (including hand missals and altar cards), in its earlier versions, and in the Ordinary Form missal. Those essential truths of our Faith are made more manifest when the words, punctuation marks, and gestures chosen are more precise.

It leads us to conclude that liturgical changes help our souls when they express better the invisible realities offered to our faith for our salvation. Those realities are that Christ died for us—the Mass is His Sacrifice reenacted—and that the Consecration formulas make Christ truly present in the Host and Chalice. Those truths will never change. They are immutable. They are necessary for all men. No salvation will ever be secured at the expense of those truths. The criterion to assess any change in our earthly liturgies is whether it helps our intellects understand those truths more clearly and our wills to desire them more ardently as goods.

No words uttered by men on earth are loaded with a greater power than those of Consecration at Holy Mass. Through the lips of the priest celebrant, the God-Man, Jesus Christ, changes the substance of bread into that of His Body and the substance of wine into that of His Precious Blood. No change greater than that one occurs in the world, whereby God makes Himself physically present among His people. Paradoxically, this greatest of events escapes our physical senses. They are incapable of reaching beyond the externals. Our eyes still see what looks like bread and wine after the Consecration. Our souls, though, detect the momentous change, when guided by faith. Faith is the key.

In the liturgy of the Mass, therefore, the selection criterion for every word and gesture, every silence and sound, every shape, color, and scent must be to improve our faith. This explains the deepest care showed by Holy Mother Church for all that pertains to the offering of Holy Mass. But faith is not a vague sentiment subjectively interpreted. Faith is a theological virtue whose divine object, God, is the same for all men. As regards Holy Mass, faith teaches us that on the Catholic altar, in every unbloody reenactment of His unique Sacrifice of Calvary, the Divine Spouse delivers Himself anew to apply the saving merits of His Passion and death to the members of His Mystical Body, the Church. Reconciled with God through the Sacrifice of His Son, Jesus, we men are consequently brought closer to one another as brethren, children of the same Father.

In proportion with our faith, then, we receive the blessed fruit of a vertical reconciliation with God, and this, in turn, allows a horizontal reconciliation among men. We are expected and entitled to pay the greatest attention to the words and gestures used in the Missal to guide our faith. Language has its own rules, which apply objectively, whether in a love poem by Shakespeare or in the Church's own love canticle to her Savior. Everyone holds Shakespeare as a most eloquent interpreter of the human heart and condition. Many students may strive to imitate the Bard's talent. But very few, if any, will match his literary genius. Why is that?

It is because their choice of words expresses human truths with less precision, strength, and beauty than his. The same applies to the Missal as regards *divine* truths. Some words express invisible truths more convincingly than others. With due reverence for the authority of the Church in promulgating liturgical texts, assessing the greater or lesser efficacy of a word or of a punctuation mark helps us better understand how our faith in the Sacrifice of Christ and in His Real Presence after the Consecration is fostered — or hindered.

As I stated at the beginning of this chapter, I readily admit that the liturgy may change. In fact, the liturgy is a work in progress until the end of time. It accompanies us on our journey toward judgment and eternity. After Christ's glorious return at the end of history, once we have been established in the everlasting possession of God (as we pray for), the liturgy will cease to be subject to change, like our souls. We will worship the Lamb who stands as slain, as described in the book of Revelation, the Apocalypse. But since no intercession or petition will be needed anymore, nor any application of Christ's merits for our improvement, the liturgy in Heaven will not be Holy Mass.

As St. Thomas Aquinas teaches: "The Saints who will be in heaven will not need any further expiation by the priesthood of Christ, but having expiated, they will need consummation through Christ Himself, on Whom their glory depends."[36] May this be a further incentive to make an ever more fruitful use of the prayers of the Missal while there is time. May we cherish in particular its sacred core, the Consecration formulas whereby the Lord sacrificially comes among us to lead us back to the Father as loving brethren.

---

[36] *Summa theologiae* III, q. 22, art. 5.

11

Holy Mass as the Measure of Motion

Heavenly and Earthly Measurements

Years ago, I used to offer Mass (according to the traditional Roman Missal) for Mother Teresa's Sisters, the Missionaries of Charity, in London. When visiting the sick in India, those Sisters would evaluate distances neither in metric nor in imperial measurements, but in Ave Marias. One can imagine an instruction to a new Sister: "You will have time to pop in at poor Mrs Aaradhka's, as she lives only three decades from the convent."

We, in turn, may ask ourselves: What frame of reference do we apply to our lives? If, according to Aristotle, "time is the measure of motion" (i.e., a change of any sort, including qualitative), then what rhythm do we choose to measure the pace of our existence? Several are offered us. Under difficult economic circumstances, many people plan from one monthly paycheck to the next, as long as one does not lose his job, please God. Or, on a lighter note: from one football game to the next; or from the winter sales to the summer sales. Or, on a shorter basis, from one Saturday-evening entertainment at one's favorite pub to the next.

In the same Sisters' sacristy in Southwark, a simple reminder was pinned on the wall above the table where the vestments were laid ready before Holy Mass. It read as follows: "Holy Priest of God, remember to offer this Mass as if it were your first Mass, your last Mass, your only Mass." For many of us, practicing Catholics, the measure of our lives may be Sunday Mass. We thus live from one Sunday Mass to the next. Such appears to be the true pulse in the Mystical Body of Christ, the Church. Every Sunday in particular, the whole Church commemorates the Resurrection of her Lord, Savior, and Spouse, Jesus Christ. Then, in the Eucharistic Sacrifice, the redeeming Blood is sent to and through us, Christ's members, irrigating the entire Body.

Each of us, if adequately prepared, is thus united to the Savior in an embrace of faith, the most intimate a soul can ever experience here on Earth. The deeper one appreciates this truth, the more one realizes the centrality of the Mass in one's daily life. Gradually, gently, the time unit adjusts from Sunday Mass to *any* Mass. One day, the soul realizes, as if awakening, that it simply needs *daily* Mass. And to her surprise, rather than being frightened by this discovery, the soul finds herself filled with deferential desire.

Consecutive Masses

On All Souls' Day (and at Christmas), the liturgy of the Church allows us to reach deeper into this truth. Traditionally, every priest may offer three Requiem Masses on All Souls' Day, so as to shower upon the suffering souls in Purgatory the merits of Christ's redeeming Sacrifice. A lot could be said about the scriptural riches of this set of three Requiem Masses, each of them with its proper Epistle, Gospel, and

Collect. But in this instance, it is the rubrics we are interested in, and they refer to "the priest who, on the feast of the Nativity of the Lord or on the Commemoration of all the Faithful departed, offers two or three Masses without interruption, that is, without leaving the altar."[37]

When starting with the "Introibo ad altare Dei" of the second Requiem, right after the Last Gospel of the first Requiem, the repetitiveness still feels unfamiliar, or even a bit heavy—although happily assumed, for the sake of the holy souls. But from the Consecration of the second Mass and, even more, when starting the third Mass, something mysterious happens in the sensitivity of the celebrant and of the congregation. The reiteration of the same liturgical gestures and words for the third time in an hour is now freed from any suggestion of artificiality. The shortsighted suspicion of a burdensome circularity has similarly vanished. Instead, one has entered a dimension where simply the Mass is the measure of motion. The liturgical offering of the Eucharistic Sacrifice has by then become the prevalent unit of reference to time and space. All that the memory recalls from before the Mass in progress is another Mass, and before that previous Mass, still another one. A strange feeling thus arises, not of dizziness but rather of acuteness: that there is no obvious reason why the repetition of the Offering should ever end—just as, in normal circumstances, one does not envisage that a sequence of sixty minutes may not follow the present hour, and again and again until the consummation of ages.

During this third consecutive Requiem, therefore, the Mass ceases to appear as an action performed among others

---

[37] *Ritus Servandus* XIV.

in the course of a day or a week; rather, it reveals itself as that which it truly is: the rhythm of Redemption. The continuous flow from the words "plenum gratiae et veritatis," concluding the Last Gospel, to "Introibo ad altare Dei" at the beginning of the next Mass henceforth appears as the medium essential to any genuine progress. The duration of that third Mass feels like that of the gyrating of oars in and out of water: each strike—each Mass—brings the ship nearer to the Ocean, that is, to eternity as one rows down a river of grace.

Holy Mass, the Pace of Our Lives

Attending three such consecutive low Masses and experiencing this truth helps our soul realize that a day when one has not attended—or offered—Holy Mass is deficient, in inverse proportion to the legitimacy of our impediments in God's eyes. We may assess how genuine our given obstacles are by asking ourselves if that weekday without Holy Mass is for us a grief, or a relief, or goes unnoticed. If we do not go to Mass on a weekday (not of obligation), let us deplore it, not ignore it. Otherwise, although we are clearly not breaking any precept of the Church, our hindrances may well prove to have been pretexts, when our soul shall stand in the light of Love Incarnate.

Our Blessed Lord calls each of us to the aspersion of His Precious Blood shed for our purification and to the sharing of His immaculate flesh pierced for our liberation, as reenacted at every Mass. The more regularly we attend (with devotion), the more fruitfully His merits work in us and in those for whom we intercede. If we cannot travel bodily to God's altar some weekday, surely no walls, no strikes, no traffic jams, no overdraft, no sickness will stop our souls. So let us check in our local parish or community bulletin to see what time Holy Mass is offered, and in which church, and let us unite our hearts with the redeeming Offering at that moment, through a spiritual communion. This simple practice will help us reveal the Eucharistic Sacrifice as the true center of our lives. Please God, the daily obstacles between our lips and the Sacred Host will diminish in number and in size like shadows, as the Sun of Justice and Mercy rises in the hands of His priest: "Ecce Agnus Dei, ecce qui tollit peccata mundi."

12

Light the Beacons!

Homily pronounced by Fr. Armand de Malleray, FSSP, at the First Solemn High Mass in England of Fr. Ian Verrier, FSSP, at St. James Church in London, on June 20, 2015.

Dear newly ordained Fr. Verrier,
 Just give up! It is all lost. Go and hide. We are vanquished. Christianity is over. Our time is gone. Anyone with eyes to see will agree. Greater than waves, tsunamis, rather, surge against life, against common sense, against freedom, and against innocence! See the crimson tide of abortion; the green tide of Islam; the pink tide of inversion; the black tide of pornography; and as a deadly mix of all others, the fluorescent tide of political correctness.

Coming fast upon us, down those evil waves, like mighty hordes of surfers, the enemy conquers our parliaments, our tribunals, our universities, our media, our hospitals, our barracks, our schools, our workplaces, our bakeries, even our homes—and what of our churches? No one is there to protect us. Our martyrs are long gone. Our confessors and doctors are dumb. Our virgins are mocked. Our leaders are shy or unsure. And *we* ... We are weak. We are selfish. We are lazy. We are afraid.

The Cleanup Chapter

Dear Fr. Verrier, more than once you crossed the Channel with many English pilgrims, to take part in the annual Pilgrimage of Christendom, from Notre-Dame Cathedral in Paris to Notre-Dame Cathedral in Chartres. You admired the glorious procession of hundreds of chapters, each carrying its embroidered banner with its local saint and its shining cross, singing canticles along the seventy-mile hallowed path to the medieval shrine of Chartres!

What you may have missed, however, is the "Cleanup Chapter." That little group of volunteers walks at the very end of the one-mile-long column. After the twelve thousand pilgrims have walked through fields and woods, that lowly party follows. They remember what an amazing sight those thousands were—now vanished as a dream! And the small Cleanup Chapter closes the column, dutifully picking up any paper, any empty cans or wrappers (or occasionally rosary beads) fallen from the pilgrims' hands. What is the ambition of the Cleanup Chapter? It is to leave the place neat and tidy, when the tiny silhouette of the last Catholic will have shrunk down to the size of a dot on the gray horizon. The Cleanup Chapter prides itself on leaving no trace behind: no one would ever guess that a Catholic army once boldly trod along that road.

Catholics worldwide in 2015, those with eyes to see, feel very much like the Cleanup Chapter. We see our parishes merged, our churches shut down, our seminaries, convents, and novitiates sold to developers, our schools de-Catholicized.

We quietly withdraw. Even as we die, we must be careful not to rock the boat. Let us vanish in a gentlemanly way, as the world sneers at us: "Farewell, miserable rearguard, and good riddance!" So, should we not give up? Should we not give in?

Putting on Our Faith Glasses

No. *That* was the horizontal vision, not the transcendent one. It was what the flesh tells us—not the Faith. Fr. Verrier, you would not be sitting in our midst as celebrant; you would not soon stand at the altar to offer the Holy Sacrifice, if you shared that deceptive vision. Dear friends, if we adhered to it ourselves, we must have misplaced our supernatural glasses. When we find them again—our proper *faith* glasses; when we focus on what escapes our eyes of flesh but not our souls—*this* is what we will see. *What* indeed, do you ask?

We will see that we belong to One who has already won the battle on our behalf. It was on Good Friday, on Mount Golgotha. He is our Head, and we are His Mystical Body, the Church. He is our Head, in Latin *caput*, whence also "captain." And our Captain will soon return, visibly. The end of time is near, for Him to whom one thousand years are like a day.

We belong to His Church, spread across time even more powerfully than across space. Here below, we only see the militant or pilgrim fringe of His Church, with a mere 1.2 billion known. But much more numerous and helpful are the suffering souls in Purgatory, who are already holy and will intercede for us when their purification is ended, if not earlier. In Heaven now, without interruption, billions of saints and trillions of holy angels petition on our behalf the adorable Trinity, led in intercession by the Most Holy Mother of God.

Spies of the Lord

With them, we are Christ's holy army. We are still on earth, yes. But we are not forgotten: we are sent. We are not lagging behind: we are scouting out. We are not the *rearguard*: we are the *vanguard*! We are the Lord's gentle spies.

Spies? Indeed! Remember how, in the Old Testament, after forty years of wandering in the desert, Joshua sent spies to reconnoiter the Promised Land, ahead of the Hebrew army, still encamped east of the River Jordan: "Josue the son of Nun sent from Setim two men, to spy secretly: and said to them: Go, and view the land and the city of Jericho. They went and entered into the house of a woman that was a harlot named Rahab, and lodged with her" (Josh. 2:1).

As the spies found refuge in the house of the prostitute Rahab, who was spared for her faith when Jericho fell, in our turn we spread the Good News among alien folk. We mark those of goodwill with the sign of the Lord, so that they may be saved, when the army will take possession of the land. We are the emissaries of the liberation forces. We have but little time to enroll as many as will trust in the Word who sent us and who guides us daily.

What are we? We are not agents of subversion because evil is chaos and the peace we bring is the tranquility of order. We are the spies of love, under the nose of hatred. We are busy smuggling mercy. We plot freedom. We inject grace. Weak and few as we may seem, we rely on apocalyptic backup in Heaven. Angels and saints listen to us, poor pilgrims that we are across our vale of tears. When our knees touch the ground below, one million hands join in prayer on high. When our hands join in prayer below, one *billion* wings spread above to shield us. Such is the Communion of Saints. All the baptized partake in this wondrous power. All of us are spies of the Great King on high, preparing His people for the liberation to come. Such is, dear friends, our shared mandate through Holy Baptism. Such is our brotherly pride.

Associate Captains

But the King, our Captain, has willed to imprint special powers in selected agents. He has made them head spies, associate captains, and chief forerunners of His final advent. Who are those, you ask? You should know. They are here. They live among us. They are the *priests*. The priests of God. Our priests.

Leaving seminary like Fr. Verrier a fortnight ago, on the day of their ordination they jump in the dark, through the night of sinful worldliness. They land behind enemy lines: not at random, but upon targets assigned by Chief Command (i.e., the Holy See and our shepherds, the bishops). They are thoroughly trained in the arts of God's grace. And what do you think is their first action once landed, and their last? They light the beacons! They activate a signal of infinite magnitude: the Holy Sacrifice of the Mass. Such is the command they received from Christ Himself: "I am come to cast fire on the earth; and what will I, but that it be kindled?" (Luke 12:49).

At each Holy Mass, the priest acts *in persona Christi*. The priest lets the divine Captain communicate His own infinite merits to all of us sinners. Out of the tyranny of the devil, the prince of this world, wounded souls are drawn into the Eucharistic light. Shivering souls are led to the warmth of the Eucharistic *fire*. From on high, the liberation army observes the radiance beaming from every altar on earth. Just as, on a clear summer night, we look up at the stars and wish we were there — reciprocally, from on high saints and angels look downward at the constellation of Masses across our dark world, and soon they will be here, visibly.

When the King's armies enter the land, on the day of wrath, those found within the Eucharistic shelters shall be spared. Like Rahab, they will have life, on account of their faith and good works. But as we examine our consciences, we admit that even lovers of the Eucharist need guidance and encouragement! And those still alien to the Eucharist need witnesses and teachers. Hence, I ask you: Where will we find such men?

The World Needs Priests

It is God's will that all should be saved. To that end, our divine Captain demands priests. With trembling, then, but with joy, today I call in His name. I call for priests. I call for holy sacrificers to offer *in persona Christi* not "the blood of goats, or of calves" (Heb. 9:12) but that of the Immaculate Lamb. I call for men. I call for associate captains. I call for God's commandos. But note that I am not calling for *supermen*. I am not calling for geniuses and heroes, as if natural skills could suffice for such a sacred enterprise. Before desiring any particular skills, I am calling for those whom Christ destines to be configured to Him: "meek, and humble of heart" (Matt. 11:29).

Listen to me then, men; future *men of God*. Your training will be gradual, brotherly, deep, and rewarding. Your weapons will be humility, prayer, joy, knowledge, purity, trust in God, good humor, discipline, endurance, and fraternity. Soon enough, you will be airborne. After takeoff and a seven-year flight, you will jump into the darkness of the world, like Fr. Verrier just a fortnight ago. You will descend with the parachute of grace and, landing according to plan, you will light the beacons. You will offer Holy Mass: "Introibo ad altare Dei!"

On the occasion of this First Solemn High Mass of our newly ordained priest back in England, I say to you, dear young men: Come undercover! Come underground, as God's secret emissaries! Come and exfiltrate souls from the entanglements of sin! Come and increase the number of the elect, through the fecundity of God's grace. Do you wish you could reply yes though you still feel weak? Then listen to the great Apostle St. Paul, the Doctor of the Nations; listen to what God told him: " 'My grace is sufficient for thee; for power is made perfect in infirmity.' Gladly therefore will I glory in my infirmities" — St. Paul then concluded — "that the power of Christ may dwell in me" (2 Cor. 12:9). Men, rise: join the *vanguard*.

Conclusion

In conclusion dear friends, let us renew our commitment as the gentle spies of Christ. Let us put on our supernatural glasses and focus on what escapes the eyes of our body but not those of our soul! Let us walk bravely, even amid the flames of vice, witnessing God's sanctity. Let us light up and make known the Eucharistic beacons, casting away the shadows of despair. Let us not rely on our skills, for we are useless servants but, poorly or richly endowed, let us do our utmost, and God will grant victory! Though we are but a few scattered emissaries, across the river Jordan, on the other side of time, the formidable armies of God are on the move!

Look! See the celestial legions of England and of Wales! See how they watch our humble scouting, while with our feeble hands we mark God's elect. See the mighty officers on high, about to set foot across the water and lead their battalions down to our earthly shores. See Alban and Augustine! See Bede and Cuthbert! See Chad, Hugh, and Thomas! The end is near. They are coming! See Winifred and Ethelreda! See Simon Stock, the gracious Carmelite! Hold the line, they are on their way! See the Pearl of York, Margaret Clitherow and Margaret Pole, both saintly mothers of priests! Stand your ground; they are here! See John Fisher and Thomas More, the columns of faithful England! See Campion and Mayne, the gallant missionaries! See John Henry Newman and Dominic Barberi!

But most of all, look at the fair one, awaiting the return of her Dowry to her, for her Son's glory: watch the Mother of God, the Most pure and chaste, our Mother through grace. "Thou art beautiful, O my love, sweet and comely as Jerusalem: terrible as an army set in array" (Cant. 6:3). On our behalf, almightily, she begs. Under her queenship, let us toil gladly and prepare the coming of her Son, Jesus, the Prince of Peace. He is on the move with His armies. He is coming to rescue us. He is here: "Ecce Agnus Dei, ecce qui tollit peccata mundi!"—"Behold the Lamb of God, behold Him who taketh away the sins of the world!"

About the Author

Fr. Armand de Malleray, FSSP, left France in 1994 after completing a master's degree in modern literature at the University of the Sorbonne in Paris. After teaching French at the military academy in Budapest, Hungary, he joined the Priestly Fraternity of St. Peter (FSSP) in 1995 in Bavaria, where he was ordained in 2001.

Fr. de Malleray's first priestly assignment was in London. He has served in England since, apart from five years in Switzerland, then in an administrative position at his Fraternity's headquarters. Since 2008, he has been the editor of *Dowry*, the quarterly magazine of his Fraternity in the United Kingdom and Ireland. Several articles originally published in *Dowry* are included in this book. Fr. de Malleray also authored the *Art for Souls* series, which presents the Catholic Faith through Christian paintings.

This book is based on the author's preaching experience, especially as chaplain to the international Juventutem youth movement since its inception in 2004 (www.juventutem.org) and to their London group since 2015. Eucharistic devotion holds pride of place in the movement, as reflected in the Juventutem logo: a monstrance. With the Juventutem young adults, Fr. de Malleray took part in the World Youth Days in Cologne, Sydney, Madrid, and Krakow. At those gatherings, Juventutem worked hard to secure official recognition for the Extraordinary Form of the Roman rite, centered on the Holy Sacrifice of the Mass. What was in 2005 in Cologne a sensational precedent has since become an expected and valued component of Word Youth Day.

Fr. de Malleray gave talks on the Holy Eucharist at the International Eucharistic Congresses of Quebec City (2008) and Dublin (2012) and to Eucharistic ministers in the Portsmouth Diocese (on Eucharistic fragments and concomitance). By appointment from his superiors in the FSSP, since 2007 the author has been chaplain to the Confraternity of St. Peter, a nearly seven-thousand-strong international prayer network fostering vocations to the priesthood. Lastly, each year, Fr. de Malleray gives systematic retreats on the Holy Eucharist and other topics to laity and clergy alike. In preparation for Adoremus, the National Eucharistic Congress in Liverpool, England (September 7–9, 2018), he gave a series of lectures on the Holy Eucharist that were advertised by the Liverpool Archdiocese and broadcast on his Fraternity's Internet channel, LiveMass. Since 2015, he is the rector of St Mary's Shrine in Warrington, in the Liverpool Archdiocese.

Other works by Fr. de Malleray:

Spirituality

Meditations on the Stabat Mater (London, UK: Catholic Truth
Society, 2022)

Fiction

Near Missed Masses (Waterloo, ON: Arouca Press, 2021)

Essays

X-Ray of the Priest in a Field Hospital (Waterloo, ON: Arouca
Press, 2020)

Ego Eimi: *It is I – Falling in Eucharistic Love* (original edition in
Ireland: Lumen Fidei, 2018)

Art Commentaries

Italian Renaissance, Art for Souls, CD-ROM (Versailles, France:
Rejoyce, 2004)

Caravage, l'art pour l'âme, CD-ROM (Versailles, France: Rejoyce, 2001)

La Tour, l'art pour l'âme, CD-ROM (Versailles, France: Rejoyce,
2000)

Sophia Institute

Sophia Institute is a nonprofit institution that seeks to nurture the spiritual, moral, and cultural life of souls and to spread the gospel of Christ in conformity with the authentic teachings of the Roman Catholic Church.

Sophia Institute Press fulfills this mission by offering translations, reprints, and new publications that afford readers a rich source of the enduring wisdom of mankind.

Sophia Institute also operates the popular online resource CatholicExchange.com. *Catholic Exchange* provides world news from a Catholic perspective as well as daily devotionals and articles that will help readers to grow in holiness and live a life consistent with the teachings of the Church.

In 2013, Sophia Institute launched Sophia Institute for Teachers to renew and rebuild Catholic culture through service to Catholic education. With the goal of nurturing the spiritual, moral, and cultural life of souls, and an abiding respect for the role and work of teachers, we strive to provide materials and programs that are at once enlightening to the mind and ennobling to the heart; faithful and complete, as well as useful and practical.

Sophia Institute gratefully recognizes the Solidarity Association for preserving and encouraging the growth of our apostolate over the course of many years. Without their generous and timely support, this book would not be in your hands.

www.SophiaInstitute.com
www.CatholicExchange.com
www.SophiaInstituteforTeachers.org

Sophia Institute Press is a registered trademark of Sophia Institute.
Sophia Institute is a tax-exempt institution as defined by the
Internal Revenue Code, Section 501(c)(3). Tax ID 22-2548708.